Praise

'Having experienced first-hand how challenging transformation programmes can be for any organisation, this book is packed with wise insights and practical advice on designing and running such programmes. It all starts with the humility to accept that what you are setting out on is very different to what an organisation is used to doing, so learning from others is key to your success. In this book, Gary presents a goldmine of these rich learnings – actioning them is down to you.'
   —**David Clamp**, Founder of the Camelot Network and SENSE Consortium

'This book contains a lifetime of knowledge from a highly experienced transformation specialist. If you are a project sponsor, decision maker, manager or team member, read it and increase the chances of having far better outcomes for your projects and programmes.'
   —**Tony Tarquini**, Insurance Industry Advisor

'In a world that is getting ever faster, it's important to go slow, to take stock before proceeding to change. This book covers all the aspects to consider, based on theory and years of practical experience, before embarking on a transformation programme.'
   —**Hélène Stanway**, Non-Executive Director, Insurance Industry Advisor and President of SENSE Consortium

'Digital transformation is a vast and complex subject area with many potential pitfalls for the uninitiated. In this book, Gary provides valuable insights, practical advice and ways to think about it that will help leaders adopt the right approach to achieving success in their digital transformation endeavours.'

—**Tim Ellis**, CEO of The Digital Transformation People and Talent Match

'What *is* the best approach for leaders to ensure that fundamental changes to the ways a business operates actually get done, never mind deliver on the promises made? It's such a vital question with so many different answers, blueprints, methodologies, silver bullets... and the rest! What we know is that technology is not the answer, however comforting that long-lived illusion might have been. So, what is? Programmes fail because the firm has paid insufficient attention to being brilliant at the art and science of collaboration. Gary has set out to practically bridge this gap with an accessible, grounded approach designed to harness the expertise, energy and collaborative muscle of every function, from specification to post-implementation review. It's much needed.'

—**Shân Millie**, The Accidental Teccie, expert in tech and data value generation in financial services

'Perspective, pacy, punchy, practical. Gary has rich experience and presents it in an entertaining and memorable manner. While there is no silver bullet for transformation, there are many golden nuggets of experience and advice in this book. Great read cover to cover, to dip into or return to.'

—**Mark Simpson**, Founder of Resilient Changing

'There are lots of books and papers published on leading organisations through transformational change, and most approach things from a theoretical perspective. I enjoyed reading this book because Gary shares his personal experience of leading organisations on such a journey. As such, this book is full of practical and pragmatic guidance that you can easily apply to help you successfully navigate what can often be choppy waters.'

—**Tony Lockwood**, Founder of The Transformation Leaders Hub

'A practical book on transformational change that will make you reconsider what you are doing and how you are doing it and change your approach immediately. Easy to read, much harder to implement, this book is full of advice that will set you on a transformation path with a much greater chance of success.'

—**Karen Stanford**, COO of GreenKite Associates

Enjoy the read!

Best wishes

Gerry

A
TRANSFORMATION
LENS

The Savvy Business Leader's Approach
To Transformational Change

GARY BURKE

R^ethink

First published in Great Britain in 2023 by
Rethink Press (www.rethinkpress.com)

Contents

Introduction

As a business leader you'll be used to making decisions, and deciding to transform your organisation and undertake a strategic transformation programme is one of the biggest you can make. You may be the person or team member making key initial decisions regarding strategy, objectives and investment. Or you may have a leadership role in the shaping, execution and delivery of the transformation programme itself, perhaps as the programme sponsor or director.

This book is primarily aimed at leaders with accountability and responsibility for successfully delivering strategic transformation programmes but who have limited experience of transformational change. However, it would also benefit anyone involved in the

1

transformation journey including project and pro-gramme professionals, key business stakeholders (who are likely to be the recipients of change), as well as solution providers – vendors and resellers – whose products are often key enablers to transformation. It's not a 'how to manage a transformation programme' guide – there is ample material available on that topic. It's more a 'how to avoid the board meeting where you need to discuss what's gone wrong, the huge sum of money you've already spent, and how to get things back on track' guide.

Whatever your role may be, the investment made in the transformation initiative will define the organ-isation's direction and shape its operation and performance for years to come – so it's important to get it right. But getting it right is more involved than you may realise. Business, digital or any other flavour of transformation is a bit like an iceberg. You may only be aware of a fraction of what's involved, but there's a lot that needs to be understood and considered that isn't immediately obvious or visible – the stuff which you really need to be aware of before you start your journey to avoid ending up with the transformation programme equivalent of the *Titanic*.

This book will help you to navigate that journey and avoid the transformation icebergs. It will allow you to better understand and view transformational change in a more holistic way, through a transformation lens, so it can be approached correctly and consequently executed and delivered successfully, saving you a lot of pain, possible reputational damage, and potentially millions in the process.

My career started on an actuarial path, but I was drawn to the transformation and change space where I've worked since the mid-nineties. It's the interplay between strategy, risk, people, culture, process and technology that I find absolutely fascinating.

I've worked across multiple business sectors in a variety of programme, consultancy and head of change roles, predominantly in the UK, but also in Europe, Bermuda and the USA, where I've seen things, good, bad and ugly, from all sides of the 'transformation fence' – client, consultancy and solution provider. Over the years I've been involved in multimillion-pound initiatives, including turning around failed programmes and helping organisations large and small to shape and deliver transformational change.

But I've become increasingly concerned at the continued rate of transformation programme failures, where they significantly underperform and don't deliver anywhere near the benefits they should. It's unnecessary and wholly avoidable, and I'm passionate about addressing this by increasing the awareness and understanding of transformational change, the impact it can have on all areas of the organisation, and how it can be approached, executed and delivered successfully.

My goal is to enable you to look at transformational change in a different way so you can make better informed decisions and be successful. Undertaking any sort of transformation is complex, and it's imperative that you go into it with your eyes wide open, fully understanding what you're letting yourself in for.

This book provides insight into the things you should know before you start your transformation journey, including what your organisation can and should do before formally engaging solution providers and armies of consultants, as well as how to avoid being exploited by less-than-scrupulous operators. This will enable you to be better prepared for when you do engage third parties, and so reduce programme risks and costs.

Some of the thoughts, concepts and techniques shared here may seem familiar, whereas others are drawn from my own experience – practices that I've found effective in conveying important points and establishing a solid foundation for transformational change.

In Chapter One, we'll cut to the chase and start by describing the two root causes of transformation programmes not being fully successful, or even failing completely. We'll then explore the approach that needs to be taken for them to be more successful. Chapters Two and Three look at what transformation is and isn't, and who's typically involved in doing it. Chapters Four to Six focus on the transformation journey – its components and how they interact with one another – with Chapters Seven and Eight looking at aspects of failure. Chapter Nine outlines some basic principles of best and good practice that should be considered for any type of change initiative, transformational or not. Last, we'll look at why a transformation lens should be applied and how this can be achieved.

Some of the chapters have QR codes that link to short videos, which bring some of the key points to life.

I hope you enjoy reading and watching.

1
Avoiding The Transformation Iceberg

In this chapter we:

- Dive straight in and identify the two root causes that need to be addressed for transformation success

- Discuss the consequences of not sufficiently addressing the root causes

- Consider how to measure the effectiveness of transformational change

Scan the QR code to watch the accompanying video.

If you look at any of the hundreds of case studies and reports produced over the years that focus on why transformation initiatives have failed, or not been anywhere near as successful as expected, you'll find the common reasons include:

- Unclear goals, lack of a shared direction
- Lack of buy-in from senior management
- Lack of expertise
- Unclear starting point, starting with technology
- Not understanding customer needs, ignoring customer experience
- Setting too fast a pace and not bringing people with you, not engaging with people
- Not changing the culture, internal resistance
- Assuming transformation is a one-off activity
- Not being able to measure success

Combinations of these reasons come up time and time again. But if they've been known about for years, and they have, why do they still occur? Are these really the root causes, or are they just symptoms of something more fundamental?

Undertaking a transformation initiative is a big deal, and given the importance, impact and costs likely to be involved, leaders will generally have the best intentions when setting out on any transformation journey and actively seek to do the right things – but something obviously isn't working. We'll explore this throughout the book, but for starters we'll look at the underlying issues, the two root causes that need to be addressed for your transformation programme to be successful. These are:

- Root Cause 1 – A lack of understanding of what transformational change involves and its impact on the organisation

- Root Cause 2 – Inappropriate capability to deliver transformational change

And these root causes can be addressed by:

- Aligning your understanding of transformational change with your appetite for it and your expectations of it

- Aligning your understanding of transformational change with your capability to deliver it

Aligning understanding, appetite and expectations

The primary root cause is simply a *lack of understanding* of what transformational change actually means and involves.

Depending on the drivers for transformation, the leadership team will have a certain appetite for the amount of transformational change that it is comfortable with and which the organisation can support. This appetite for change will align with your initial (possibly incorrect) understanding of what it involves, the impact it will have on all areas of the organisation, and the challenges and complexities that may be faced. From this alignment, expectations will develop and crystallise around costs, benefits, effort and timescales, Figure 1 (left).

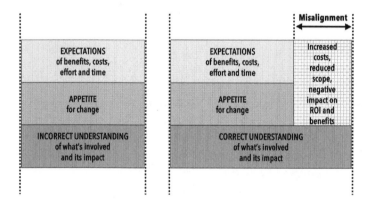

Figure 1: The consequences of not having the correct initial understanding of transformational change.

But, at some stage during the transformation programme, the correct understanding will become apparent, Figure 1 (right). Any misalignment of understanding and appetite will need to be bridged, either by increasing your appetite for change and the accompanying costs, or by reducing scope and ambition to stay within your original appetite and budget. In extreme cases, the programme may no longer be viable but, at the very least, the expected benefits won't be realised and the business case and return on investment (ROI) will be compromised.

To avoid falling at the first hurdle, you need to ensure that you genuinely understand what transformational change involves and that your understanding is aligned to your appetite for it.

Aligning understanding and capability

The second root cause relates to aligning your understanding of transformational change with the capability to deliver it. There are two sides to this:

- Expertise and experience
- Motive

Expertise and experience

You will assign or engage the capability that can perform and deliver your transformation programme in line with your initial understanding, Figure 2 (left). If this understanding is incorrect, the capability that you engaged may not have the necessary skills and experience to do this, leaving you with a capability gap, Figure 2 (right). This may have serious implications for the success of your transformation programme.

 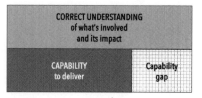

Figure 2: The correct understanding is needed to get the appropriate capability.

An analogy... if you enjoy cooking and entertaining, you'd no doubt be quite comfortable hosting a dinner party for six friends, Figure 3 (top), but you'd probably think twice if you were asked to host a ten-course banquet for 100 people, Figure 3 (bottom). Although this is still cooking, you'd know that the banquet is more complex and presents more challenges and requires specific skills and experience to do it properly.

Transformational change is like the banquet, and if you don't fully understand the extent of what's involved, you'll approach it as though you're cooking dinner for friends and be on the path to failure before you've even begun.

Figure 3: Cooking for friends (top)[1] vs a banquet (bottom)[2] –
both cooking, but they require different sets of skills
and experience.

So, at the very beginning of a transformation initiative, way before any formal programme exists, who
are you going to ask to produce the initial feasibility
report or high-level business case that will be used to
inform the strategic direction and investment decisions? Will it be that programme manager who has
had some great successes but has no real experience

13

of transformational change? If so, what are they going to miss? How can a business case be constructed if there isn't sufficient understanding of what's actually involved?

For key roles such as the programme director, look for someone with the right type and level of experience. For example, if implementing new technology is one of the strategic programme objectives, the programme director should have a working knowledge of that type of technology, ie its generic functionality and how it can be used. But it wouldn't be necessary or desirable for them to have in-depth knowledge of specific systems, or worse (which I've seen), specific versions of systems. That's why you have subject matter experts – they perform different roles and have different skill sets.

Another analogy… if you were looking for a conductor for an orchestra, you wouldn't expect candidates to have played or be able to play all the instruments. A conductor is there to conduct, to lead, to orchestrate. They need to understand what each instrument can do and how to get the best from all the individual elements so that they work harmoniously together. That's what the programme director is there to do.

You may of course engage external help from consultancies or system integrators (SIs), particularly if your change capability is limited. Solution providers may also have their own delivery capability or work with their preferred SIs to provide consultancy and implementation services. External companies will inevitably tell you how good their product, service or track record is, though this should always be taken with a pinch (or bag) of salt until you can verify their claims for yourself. This can sometimes be difficult to do, as references from previous clients may only be available from senior people who weren't necessarily exposed to the reality of working directly with the third party in question.

Unfortunately, instances of bad practice and poor performance don't tend to filter through to the public domain, so the possibility of history repeating itself perpetuates, ie prospective clients are often none the wiser and, by choosing some consultancies and solution providers, find themselves with inexperienced resources or poor products and, effectively, are lambs to the slaughter.

Motive

A key consideration when engaging third parties is whether they are always acting in your best interests. Are your organisation's objectives and goals fully shared by them? Is there a common agenda that all parties are fully bought into?*

You will care about approaching, executing and delivering your transformation programme in a

---

* I am, of course, assuming the other divisions and departments within your organisation do share the same goals. Although this should be the case, be aware that it may not always be so.

cost-effective way that delivers strategic goals, enables you to move to a new way of working and realises all the benefits you expect at the earliest opportunity. Figure 4 (left) illustrates this with the capability engaged fully sharing your objectives. The solution provider or consultancy on the other hand may be more interested in maximising revenue or licence fees, looking to burrow its way deeper into your organisation, sustaining ambiguity, getting as many consultants working on the programme as possible (needed or not) and not delivering anything for as long as possible, Figure 4 (right). This will be great for their revenue stream but not so good for your business case.

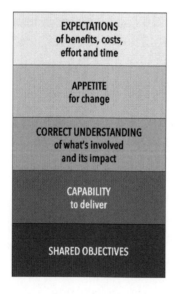 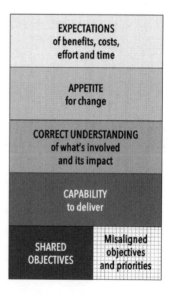

Figure 4: External parties' objectives need to align with yours so your best interests are served.

There are still too many instances of consultancies that wheel out very smart, knowledgeable and capable people during the sales process (suitably accompanied by lots of snazzy slide decks) only for the client to end up with a lot of 'consultants' with a couple of years of experience who have been on some training courses – bright people but with minimal real-world experience, and certainly not enough to have acquired the appropriate skills to understand transformational change and avoid the icebergs... and they usually incur expensive rates to boot.

I must stress that not all consultancies, SIs and solution providers are the same. Some will be exceptionally good and go the extra mile to make sure you, as their client, are genuinely looked after and they will have your best interests at heart. But others will try to exploit any naivety and lack of experience you have for their gain. The hard bit is determining which provider is which.

So, to maximise the chances of successfully transforming your organisation, you need to ensure your understanding of transformational change is aligned to your appetite for it and the capability to deliver it, Figure 5.

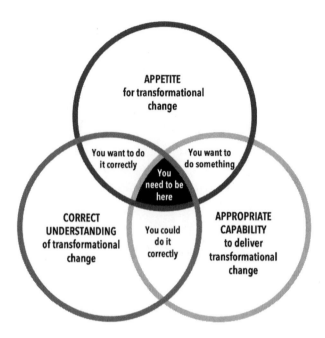

Figure 5: Alignment of understanding, appetite and capability is key to successful transformation.

LET'S TALK ABOUT... SPINNING SUCCESS

I know from my experience, and that of colleagues, where transformation programmes have gone seriously off the rails but have eventually been spun as being successful. The full story, unsurprisingly, is seldom talked about – the non-existent functionality that was originally promised, shambolic implementation methods, weak leadership, spiralling costs, the detrimental impact on the customer, and the months of costly remediation that it took to achieve 'success'.

Measuring success

This can be tricky. By potentially transforming what your organisation does and how it does it, a lot of things are likely to change. You will have your benefits case and expectations of which benefits will be realised in specific areas and when, but due to the nature of transformational change, these may be more akin to best guesses than accurate predictions.

The metrics used to gauge how your organisation is performing (pre-transformation) will vary in accuracy depending on the reliability of the data available. You may be able to state sales figures with confidence, but do you have sufficiently accurate data to understand how much it costs to onboard a new client or introduce a new product? Once reliable data can be collected, it may well show a dip in performance, for example, longer processing times or higher costs than you were experiencing pre-transformation. This does not necessarily mean that the changes made have degraded performance, it may be that the new information is accurate and your original understanding was wrong, as it was based on inaccurate data.

Be mindful that the metrics used to measure how successful any transformation initiative has been, if looked at individually, may not give you a true picture. Just as transformational change requires a holistic view and approach, measuring its success requires similar treatment, so a range of metrics and ratios across all functions should be considered. For example:

- Customer experience – eg number and type of complaints, net promoter score

- Colleague experience – eg satisfaction surveys, staff turnover, vacancy rates, absence rates

- Operating efficiency – eg production time, channel usage, error rates, service availability

- Financial performance – eg revenue, revenue per FTE, products per customer, operating costs

- Market performance – eg market share, share price

One way of demonstrating the effect transformational change has on an organisation can be seen in Figure 6, where cross-functional metrics (A–H) are represented on a spoke diagram, with the scale on each spoke varying according to the metric in question. The area bounded by the light grey dashes reflects pre-transformation values, the black dashes post-transformation – the larger the area, the bigger the improvement.

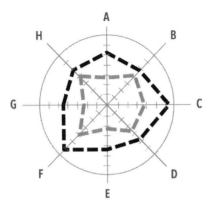

Figure 6: A range of measures is needed to determine the effect of transformational change.

Summary

Two underlying root causes – lack of understanding and inappropriate capability – give rise to the reasons typically attributed to transformation initiatives not being successful. Being aware of these, and why and how they manifest themselves, allows you to avoid them and gives your fledgling transformation initiative a much better chance of succeeding.

Taking sufficient time to genuinely understand what transformation involves and its impact on the organisation, and getting the right capability on board is time well spent. Without this understanding, you'll be flying blind. There may be pressure to 'get on with it' but having lots of resources and third parties 'doing stuff' isn't necessarily productive – a child's spinning top moves very quickly, and looks as if there's a lot going on, but it doesn't actually make any progress.

In the following chapters, we'll take a step back and look at some key concepts and components of the transformation journey, and how to approach it for its successful execution and delivery.

Key points

- The primary root cause for transformation failure is the lack of understanding of what's involved with transformational change and its impact on the organisation.

- Transformational change is complex – think banquet, not dinner party.

- External parties may not always share your goals or act in your best interests.

- Transformation requires a cross-functional and holistic approach – measuring its success requires the same.

Food for thought

- Are you aware of transformation programmes where the impact on the organisation was underestimated (and how did it affect the business case)?

- Have you used third parties who, with hindsight, should have behaved better?

- Have you ever been part of a board meeting where the 'why is this programme not going well' discussion was had?

2
Change – What Is It?

In this chapter we:

- Look at what we mean when talking about 'transformation'

- See how 'transformational change' differs from 'non-transformational change' and why it's important to know the difference

- Consider the different ends of the transformation spectrum

- Look at why it's important to be open to new ideas and different ways of thinking

When an organisation decides to do something differently, be it starting something new, doing an existing thing differently, or stopping doing something altogether, it will need to change to achieve it. However, *doing* change – identifying it, managing it and making it stick – is something that many organisations, small, large, established or scaling up, often struggle to do well.

This is particularly the case with transformational change, ie the strategic, structural stuff required to bring about a step change in operation and performance, that creates a different future and enables additional value to be created. It's the type of change that can significantly impact an organisation's business model and operating model (more on these in Chapter Four).

And here's where the challenges begin, as these three terms – transformation, business model and operating model – are not always understood as well as they need to be. And by not understanding what these terms mean – what they are and how they relate to one another – organisations can severely underestimate what's involved with transformational change and consequently the right approach and actions needed to deliver successful outcomes.

Change vs transformation

What does 'transformation' in a business context actually mean and how does that differ from 'change'?

Asking Google about transformation returned the following number of results:*

- 'What is the difference between change and transformation?' – 650 million

- 'What is business transformation?' – 846 million

- 'What is digital transformation?' – 674 million

- 'What is the difference between business transformation and digital transformation?' – 510 million

That's a lot of results, but are these questions sensible or even the right terms to be searching to provide some clarity? Moreover, what do people mean when they talk about transformation? Are they really thinking about automation or modernisation or innovation? Even if they think they're talking about transformation, are they actually referring to digitisation (converting information from analogue to digital form, eg the paperless office) or digitalisation, ie making greater use of digital tools and data?

People love to label and pigeonhole things and transformation is no different so we end up with digital, business, process, cultural, organisational, and other types and flavours of transformation, including specific function transformation such as IT (information technology), finance, and HR (human resources),

---

* At the time of writing in March 2023.

among others. But by doing this, we're looking at things through too narrow a lens. This can result in a siloed view and the unintentional imposing of artificial boundaries – virtual barriers that constrain thinking and the ability to fully appreciate and understand what's involved. In turn, this can impair and compromise the decisions being made, the right approach being determined, and the correct direction being set, all of which may result in you not achieving what you set out to do.

You may think that some authoritative reading may prove more useful, but which of the hundreds of books available on change and transformation do you start with? There is so much information available, sometimes conflicting, so how do you make sense of it all? How do you know what's genuinely useful as opposed to being overly theoretical or not appropriate for your organisation and situation? There's a big difference between what may be needed for a start-up company, for an organisation that is expanding and scaling up, and for more established national and multinational businesses with varying degrees of complexity and legacy.

Different approaches may also be required depending on what's driving the need to transform. For example, an organisation's appetite for transformation, and hence its focus and priorities, may be very different if the need for change is being driven by mandatory regulatory reasons, where there is little choice but to change, rather than cost reduction or optimisation reasons, ie discretionary change, where the organisation has much more control.

With any project or programme, the primary factors that an organisation will have to balance are typically a mix of:

- Cost – of the programme itself and post-live operational and support costs

- Quality – of deliverables, taking into account the risks involved in not fully achieving the desired quality at the outset

- Time – resource availability, how long before benefits start being realised, and the total duration of the programme

These factors are all interrelated and the drivers for change will affect how each is prioritised.

Transformation is change (but not all change is transformational)

When you change something, that thing is, of course, changed. I can change my socks or my car. I can change a business process, perhaps by automating it to improve how it's done. These changes can usually be done in relative isolation, discretely, to their own end. Once they are completed, that's it – I have fresh socks, a new car, an improved process.

In organisations, change happens all the time, but the mechanism through which change is delivered will depend on the nature and scale of the change, Table 1. Small changes may be performed within individual business areas as part of the day-to-day, business as usual (BAU) operation. As the scale and complexity of change increases, more appropriate delivery mechanisms are needed, such as projects, programmes and transformation programmes.

Table 1: The different ways in which change can be delivered

Nature and scale of change	Significant business and/ or operating model impact	Transfor- mational?	Change delivery mechanism
Very small/ small	No	No	None, generally performed as BAU activity
Small/ medium	No	No	Project
Medium/large	Some but not significant	Minor	Programme
Strategic/ structural, ie transforma- tional	Yes	Yes	Transformation programme

What the terms used in Table 1 (small, large, minor, etc) mean for your organisation is for you to decide – it isn't prescriptive but simply to help you think about the possible ways change can be delivered.

Non-transformational change is usually just referred to as 'change' and is generally made within the existing constraints of the organisation – typically limited by the technology, the skills people have, and process and organisational factors. This is illustrated in Figure 7 (top) where the box represents the organisation, and the arrows the opportunities for change within its boundaries. When change is made, it will tend to be singularly focused, often with minimal impact on areas outside of the one directly affected.

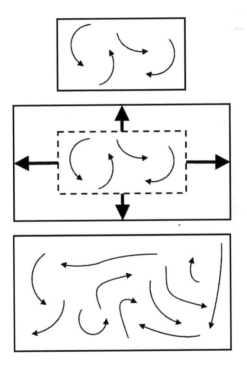

Figure 7: The opportunities for change pre-transformation (top), the effect of transformational change (middle), and the greater opportunities for change post-transformation (bottom).

With transformational change, the results and outcomes will be much wider ranging and far reaching. There will likely be a large amount of change across multiple areas. The transformation, ie the cumulative effect of all the changes, will have a structural impact on the organisation, will push the boundaries and expand, reshape and redefine the organisational playing field, Figure 7 (middle). This can enable a step change to be taken in what the organisation does – defined by its business model – and how it does it – defined by its operating model.

Transformational change should satisfy some strategic goals and provide greater scope and opportunities for future change and improvement, Figure 7 (bottom). For example, implementing or replacing a core technology platform may achieve some immediate strategic goals, such as consolidating and decommissioning legacy systems or moving to a cloud environment, but it could also enable new ways of working to be introduced. This may involve a redesign of the organisational structure, roles to be reshaped, people reskilled and upskilled, and processes reengineered.

Recognising that the initiative you're considering is transformational, rather than just changing things, and having a clear understanding of what that journey is likely to entail, is crucial to minimising the risk of transformation programme failure and to maximising the probability of success.

LET'S TALK ABOUT... CHANGE MANAGEMENT

Something that grates with me is why change management is sometimes talked about as if it's a completely separate discipline from project and programme management. As illustrated earlier in the chapter, the mechanism by which any change is delivered depends on the nature and scale of the change. The things that may be impacted by the change could include technology – what it is and how it's used – processes, organisational structure, what people do and how they do it, sales and distribution channels, the service provided to customers, and any other aspect of the organisation and its operation. Managing these aspects and ensuring that the business, its people and its customers are *appropriately* involved, communicated with, trained and prepared for the change (and that the change is properly implemented and embedded within the BAU operation), are all integral parts of managing any type of project or programme.

Change management is often described as the 'soft' or 'people side of change' and project management as the 'hard' or 'technical side of change'. Why? It strikes me as rather ironic that this distinction places an artificial boundary between change management and project/ programme management, particularly given that identifying and removing boundaries and silos is often a key part of any transformation. Still, if it helps focus minds on managing certain aspects of change, this is OK, as long as it's recognised that change management is not a completely separate thing.

Why should you care?

The reasons to transform an organisation are many. Transformation may be enabled by the introduction of new technology, or perhaps driven by merger and acquisition (M&A) activity and the integration of separate organisations into a single entity, or a root-and-branch restructure to modernise operations, or any number of other perfectly rational, well-intentioned reasons.

Change, be it small scale, large scale or transformational, is nothing new and organisations have always had to adapt to it, but the rate and pace of change now is unprecedented. There is an onslaught of change from multiple directions, including:

- New technology, artificial intelligence (AI), and disruption from new entrants

- Greater integration and interoperability, everything digital

- Dealing with legacy technology

- Increasing regulation

- Higher customer expectations and reduced customer loyalty

- Operational resilience

- Data and cybersecurity

- Environment, social and governance (ESG) and sustainability

- Equality, diversity and inclusion

- Social media

- Virtual and augmented reality

- Existential threats and disruptive events

- Social, economic and political uncertainty and instability

These are in addition to the never-ending pressure to increase revenues and minimise costs.

VUCA

The concept of VUCA[3] dates from 1985 and draws on the leadership theories of Warren Bennis and Burt Nanus from their book, *Leaders: Strategies for taking charge*[4], and helps describe the challenges of management and leadership in unpredictable conditions and situations. It was used by the United States military to help understand the state of the world after the collapse of the Soviet Union, and over recent years has increasingly been applied to the business world.

A VUCA environment is one that is:

- **V**olatile – where change is rapid and unpredictable in its nature and extent

- Uncertain – where the present is unclear and the future is uncertain

- **C**omplex – where many different, interconnected factors come into play, with the potential to cause chaos and confusion

- **A**mbiguous – where there is a lack of clarity or awareness about situations

Operating in a VUCA environment is not a desirable state as possible consequences include:

- People become demotivated and anxious.

- Individuals and organisations are overwhelmed with a toll taken on internal culture.

- Constant retraining and reshaping become a necessity.

- Huge amounts of time and effort are required just to stand still.

- The chances of making bad decisions are increased and decision-making processes become paralysed.

- Investment in long-term projects and innovations are jeopardised.

The increased use of VUCA in the business world reinforces that uncertainty and change are here to stay – it's one of the few things that organisations can be sure of about the future. It can be extremely disruptive, as the events of recent years have shown in spades, with Brexit, the global Covid-19 pandemic and war in Europe, to mention a few.

To remain competitive, organisations need to be able to respond to change effectively, adapting what they do and how they operate, and instigating and executing change swiftly and with confidence – they need agility. Organisations can no longer afford in terms of cost, time or reputation to be slow to adapt to change or to get it wrong – it needs a right-first-time response.

The transformation spectrum

There are various ways of going about transformational change and here we'll look at each end of the transformation spectrum – radical transformation and incremental transformation.

Radical transformation

An example sometimes used to differentiate between transformational and non-transformational change is that of a caterpillar transforming into a butterfly, rather than just making a bigger, faster caterpillar. But let's consider that for a moment.

One day, a caterpillar will stop eating, hang upside down from a twig and spin a cocoon. It then digests itself, releasing enzymes to dissolve all its tissues – the result is quite literally caterpillar soup. But this soup also contains groups of cells known as imaginal discs, which the caterpillar has previously grown for each of the parts it will need as a mature butterfly. These imaginal discs use the protein-rich soup to fuel the cell division required to form the wings, legs, eyes, and all the other features of an adult butterfly and, within its protective cocoon, the caterpillar radically transforms its body, eventually emerging as a butterfly.

Now, applying that sort of transformation to the corporate world, ie wholly dismantling, deconstructing and then recreating the organisation in a completely new form, is certainly at the extreme end of the spectrum. What you should take away from this though, is that the caterpillar's transformation is *the resulting effect of a series of orchestrated activities to produce a defined outcome*, albeit a rather radical one.

But the changes required to effect a transformation don't have to be so radical and so 'big bang', ie everything at once, they can be more subtle and incremental.

Incremental transformation

In 2003 British Cycling had only won one gold medal at the Olympic Games since 1908. The performance of British riders had been so underwhelming that one of the top bike manufacturers in Europe refused to sell bikes to the team because they were afraid it would hurt sales.

Dave Brailsford became performance director of British Cycling in 2003 and introduced the concept of 'marginal gains',[5] breaking down everything that involved riding a bike – the thinking being that if every aspect could be improved by 1%, the aggregation of all the improvements would lead to a significant increase in overall performance. Adjustments were made that you might expect from a professional cycling team:

- They looked at diet and exercise regimes.

- Equipment was redesigned, from saddles to optimising tyre pressures.

- They switched to indoor racing suits, which were lighter and more aerodynamic.

- They rubbed alcohol on the tyres for better grip (who knew that?!).

- Before a race, riders wore electrically heated shorts to maintain ideal muscle temperature.

- Each rider's position on the bike was analysed in a wind tunnel.

And they continued to find marginal improvements in less obvious areas:

- Different types of massage gels were tested to see which led to the fastest muscle recovery.

- A surgeon was hired to teach riders the best way to wash their hands to reduce the chances of catching a cold.

- Sleep patterns were analysed, and when staying in hotels, the team would take their own mattresses, pillows and duvets with them, all of which were hypoallergenic.

- The inside of the team truck was painted white to help spot dust particles that would normally go unnoticed but could degrade the performance of the finely tuned bikes.

As these and hundreds of other small improvements accumulated, the results were astounding. Team performance was transformed and at the Olympic Games in Beijing in 2008, the British Cycling team dominated events, winning an incredible 60% of the gold medals available. Four years later in London, they set nine Olympic records and seven world records, and in 2016 in Rio, they topped the medal table again.

Shifting mindsets

One of the most important but sometimes overlooked aspects of any transformation is the shift in thinking and mindset required. Without being open to new and different ideas and looking at things in a different way, you'll likely repeat what you've always done, including the mistakes, and end up with no real change at all.

We're not necessarily talking about radical, revolutionary, completely off-the-wall ideas, but simply being aware that there are different ways of looking at things and doing things. The following example involves Formula 1 motor racing and babies.

Formula 1 is the pinnacle of motor racing. It's a global sport with more than twenty races each year at locations across the world. Each race lasts up to two hours and covers approximately 200 miles, with speeds in excess of 200 miles per hour. Every car stops at least once for new wheels and tyres to be fitted, and if you've never seen a pit stop, it's actually a very impressive spectacle, Figure 8:

- The driver comes into the pits, stops the car in its allocated spot and the stopwatch starts.

- Mechanics place jacks under the front and rear of the car and all four wheels are lifted off the ground.

- Each of the four wheel nuts is undone and removed.

- The four old wheels and tyres are removed.

- Four new wheels and tyres are put on.

- Each of the four wheel nuts is replaced and tightened.

- The car is lowered to the ground.

- As soon as the car is on the ground, the driver is off and the watch is stopped.

The time a car is stationary is typically between two and three seconds although the world record in a race is 1.82 seconds.[6]

Figure 8: A Formula 1 pit stop.[7]

LET'S TALK ABOUT... COST VS QUALITY VS TIME

A pit stop also provides a great, although extreme, example of the compromise that usually needs to be made when doing any project or programme – the trade-off between cost, quality and time factors. There is likely to be constant tension between these factors, but in Formula 1 this isn't the case. With the potential risk and dangers involved, there is zero room for any drop in quality, and saving time is the absolute goal, so there can't be any compromise there either. This leaves cost as the only factor that can be flexed, and flexed it is, with twenty people involved in a pit stop, each with their own very specific task. Pit stops could of course be done more cheaply, for example with only five people, but this would significantly increase the time it takes, which isn't a viable option.

So where do babies come into this?

I said earlier that having the right approach, attitude and mindset, and being able to reimagine what and how things are done are key factors of transformational change. The neonatal unit at the University Hospital of Wales worked with a Formula 1 team to see how pit stop techniques could be incorporated into their work in the resuscitation of newborn babies.[8]

Although it's not immediately obvious, there are key similarities between pit stops and neonatal resuscitation, as both require a team of people to work seamlessly together in a time-critical and space-limited environment. As a result of working together, the neonatal team identified numerous changes to its ways of working, including:

- Streamlining the resuscitation trolley so equipment could be found more easily and quickly

- Mapping out a standardised floor space to clearly show the area for the team to work in, copying the idea of a customised floor map used by the race team

- Adopting new communications and analysis techniques, including greater use of hand signals rather than verbal communication

- Using video analysis to review performance following a resuscitation, with debrief meetings as standard

To identify and make these changes required a shift in thinking, a willingness to look at things in a different light, a different mindset. The desired outcome was the same as always – to resuscitate babies and minimise their long-term health complications – but how the team achieved this was reimagined.

Transformation (what it is and what it isn't)

There is a common misconception that transformation is always large scale, expensive, takes years, and is complex and hard. Of course, it can be all these things, but it doesn't have to be. Let's look at each of these.

Large scale?

No. The eventual impact on the organisation may be huge, but the changes required to effect the transformation can be small and incremental.

Expensive?

No. Lots of changes (small, medium and large) may well be expensive when aggregated, but each change or set of changes should add value, whether directly or indirectly. The right approach combined with effective leadership and management should ensure that total benefits far exceed total costs.

Takes years?

No. The complete transformation of an organisation may take years, but this doesn't mean that benefits and better outcomes can't begin to be realised in the early stages. The programme just needs to be structured and led sensibly and effectively.

Complex?

Yes. It is complex because of the number of components involved and the interaction between them. Transformation is multidimensional with a lot of moving parts. It can impact customers, products, distribution channels and value-creating activities, as well as the corporate culture, leadership and management styles, the organisational structure and governance frameworks. Then there is the effect on peoples' roles and skills, workflows and processes (including customer journeys etc), data, applications, networks and infrastructure. It can also impact the ecosystem the organisation exists and operates in if suppliers, partners and other external parties are affected.

Hard?

No. Although transformational change is complex, that doesn't automatically make it hard. There will inevitably be hard decisions along the way, and organisations don't always make it easy for themselves (see Chapter Nine) but doing anything is hard if you don't have the right experience, skills, mindset and tools.

It's also often said that transformation is all about the people – it's not. Likewise, you can't say it's all about the culture, or the technology, or any single element – it's just too narrow a view, more labelling and pigeonholing. All aspects need to be considered as there are no hard boundaries between each element. They shape and influence one another, which is why a holistic approach is required.

Does the definition of transformation really matter?

Yes, it does, but only to a point. Labelling every project or programme as one of transformation dilutes the strength of what it should mean, ie making significant strategic and structural changes to the organisation to bring about a step change in operation and performance.

Calling something 'transformation' should convey the importance of that initiative. This isn't to say non-transformational change isn't important – of course it is – but transformational change is about redefining what the organisation does and how it does it, to create a new future.

Aside from using the term 'transformation' more appropriately, the most important thing is to be clear about what it means to you. This includes:

- Having a clear purpose with clearly defined outcomes. This doesn't mean you need to have all the answers or know exactly how you're going to achieve what you want, but you do need to have a clear vision and understand what it is you want to achieve.

- Being very clear about why you want to achieve these outcomes. Is your rationale reasoned and based on appropriate research and sound data, or is it just a vanity project or the latest bandwagon to jump on?

- Using consistent language and terminology so you can describe the outcomes you want to the many parties that will be involved. This sounds basic, but if you describe the same thing in a number of different ways, it will be very hard for everyone to share the same vision and be on the same page as you.

- Recognising that what you want and what you need may not be the same thing. Is the problem you want to overcome really the problem that needs solving? Is the opportunity you want to exploit truly appropriate for your organisation at this time?

Summary

The definition of transformation is not a clear-cut thing. It's a slippery and often misunderstood term with a wide spectrum of possibilities, from the incremental to the radical, and anywhere in between. It's so much more than just implementing some shiny new technology. That may be an enabler to transformation, but transformational change also requires a shift in mindset and attitude to reimagine what the organisation does and how it does it. And, as stated at the beginning of the chapter, what I'm describing are changes to the organisation's business model and operating model, which we'll discuss further in Chapter Four.

In the next chapter though, we'll look at how change and transformational change are done, and who typically does them.

Key points

- Organisations can't afford in terms of cost, time or reputation to be slow to adapt to change or to get it wrong – it needs a right-first-time response.

- Transformation isn't something you do to an organisation – it's the resulting state following the completion of orchestrated activities to produce defined outcomes.

- Transformation is complex, but it doesn't have to be hard – anything is hard if you don't have the right experience, skills, mindset and tools.

- What you want and what you need may not be the same thing.

- Transformational change can impact all areas of an organisation, so you can't look at elements in isolation – they're all connected and it requires a cross-functional and holistic approach.

Food for thought

- Do you overuse the term 'transformation'?

- When was the last time you were involved in a truly transformational change initiative?

- Have you ever sought inspiration or used expertise from outside your immediate line of business or industry?

3
Change – Who Does It?

In this chapter we:

- Take a conceptual look at what organisations do

- See why it's important for organisations to have a change capability

- Highlight further aspects to be aware of when engaging external parties

To adapt and react swiftly and confidently to change – to have business agility – organisations need a change capability, ie the skills and resources to oversee, lead, manage and support the organisation through periods of change in a controlled and structured way.

As we looked at in Chapter Two, anything other than very small change would typically be delivered via a project or programme. However, a one-size-fits-all approach should not be taken with these – the approach needs to reflect the scale and nature of the change.

Smaller-scale change may not need to have a full-blown project set up, but just a little bit of structure, even if it's only a few rows on a spreadsheet showing key tasks, who's doing them and when they're needed by – just be sensible about it. Establishing a project or programme should not involve lots of bureaucracy and red tape, but if it does, you should review your project initiation process.

It also doesn't necessarily follow that a large company needs to have a large change capability. It just needs to be appropriate for the organisation, reflective of the nature of its business and of its propensity to change.

Organisations do three things

Conceptually, organisations, only do three things – they 'do', 'strategise' and 'change', Figure 9.

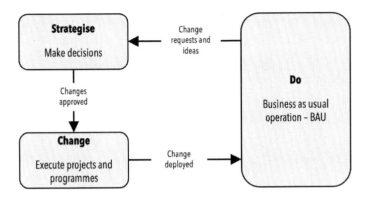

Figure 9: Conceptually, organisations only do three things.

'Do' - keep the business running

If you took a snapshot of any organisation, you would capture its activities and ways of working at that moment – its BAU state. BAU is about running the organisation and keeping it running, and comprises all the departments and teams required to do that, such as operations, IT, sales, marketing, manufacturing, finance, HR, risk, compliance, audit, legal, etc. Without any changes, BAU is a fixed, steady state that uses the organisation's existing capabilities and resources.

'Strategise' - decide whether to change

Organisations make strategic and tactical decisions to change – to do new things, stop doing things, or do things differently. Decisions about what and how to change are made all the time across all levels of an organisation. Big, strategic decisions are likely to be made at senior and executive levels, whereas a host of smaller process and continuous improvement decisions, as well as small operational business decisions are made at lower levels of the organisation.

'Change' – make and deploy changes to BAU

Once a strategic or tactical decision to change has been made, the organisation needs to act upon that decision and execute it in the most appropriate way. This may involve instigating a project or programme if the scale of change required warrants it, or the change may be small and discrete enough to be actioned directly within the area of the organisation requiring it. However, the types of change that fall into this latter category should have clearly defined parameters to avoid any unforeseen consequences.

Whatever the size of the change, the objective is to improve the BAU operation in some way. Effecting smaller change may result in being able to do something faster, more efficiently or more consistently, allowing a better service to be provided to customers and improving their experience. A larger change would ideally result in a wider range of benefits being realised across a greater number of areas.

Regardless of the size of change, it needs to be managed appropriately.

Change capability

An organisation's change capability describes:

- Who's involved in doing change – the **change team** and the resources that manage, deliver and govern change

- What activities are performed – the **change function**

- The guiding principles, policies, standards and procedures for effecting change – the **change framework**

The change team

There may be a central change team supporting all areas or, depending on the size and nature of the organisation, there may be change teams or change agents within specific functions who are involved in change activity solely within those areas. This is fine as long as any changes made don't impact other areas – but if they do, that impact needs to be appropriately understood and managed in line with the organisation's change framework.

If there is a central change team, it most probably sits in one of two places within the organisation:

- In the IT department

- Independently, occupying the space between business and technology areas

If the change function sits within the IT department, it may be too technically focused and distant from the business. Like it or not, there is often still an attitude of 'us and them' that exists between the business and IT. An IT-based change team may not have a full enough appreciation or understanding of the business operation, while the business areas may actively avoid engaging with an IT-based change team as they may be seen as *them* not *us*. This will undermine the effectiveness and benefit of any change capability.

An independent change function performed by a team sitting between the business and technology areas, perhaps supported by change agents or champions embedded within specific areas, is more likely to have better relationships with all areas. This is critical, as to truly embed change into the organisation it needs to be done *with* people, and not done *to* them.

Change teams should contain the roles and resources to effect, manage and govern change. These roles should reflect the way the organisation prefers to undertake change and may differ depending on the preference towards waterfall or agile delivery methodologies. They could, for example, include:

- Project and programme managers/directors
- Change managers
- Scrum masters and product owners
- Developers and software engineers

- Architects (business, enterprise, technical, solution, application, etc)

- Business and system analysts

- Testers and quality assurance experts

- Project management office (PMO) resources

If people from the BAU operation are seconded to work on projects, it's important to recognise that 'project mode' and 'BAU mode' are very different ways of working. In BAU mode, there are generally clear expectations and well-understood and defined activities, risks and outcomes to manage. Project mode is often the opposite, so if people are not used to working in that way, you should recognise that they may need support and time to adjust to the new way of working, ie often in an environment of uncertainty.

The change function

All change teams should be part of a connected change function that sits horizontally across the organisation, Figure 10. This function typically performs and coordinates a variety of change-related activities, including:

- Business case development

- Project and programme scoping, planning, initiation and mobilisation

- Project and programme management and reporting through the full life cycle of the initiative

- Management of risks, issues, assumptions, dependencies, costs and benefits

- Communications and internal and external stakeholder management

- Supplier and third-party engagement, relationship development and management

- Training, transition and deployment to BAU

- Embedding change within the BAU environment

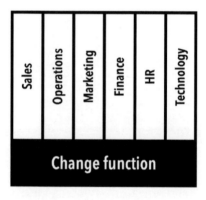

Figure 10: The change function should sit across all functions.

For larger-scale change and transformational change, activities may also include:

- Feasibility studies

- Model offices and proofs of concept (PoC)

- Requests for information (RFI) and requests for proposal (RFP)

- Solution provider and product evaluation and selection

- Involvement in contract negotiation (to provide an implementation and delivery perspective)

Along with the above, there needs to be a governance function to ensure that all activities are performed in a structured and controlled way. This is owned and managed by the PMO.

PMOs can come in many flavours, from the reactive – providing purely project and programme administration support – to those who play a more proactive role, being the beating heart of the programme. I tend to favour PMOs towards the more proactive end of the scale, ie those that have a genuinely holistic view across all project activities, with sufficient authority (and teeth!) to ensure adherence to standards.

The purpose of having standards and an agreed approach is to ensure that all change activity is undertaken in a structured and transparent manner, with accurate information available so that activities can be effectively managed and informed decisions confidently made. A good PMO adds value to any change initiative.

The change framework

The change framework describes how the organisation deals with change – how it's instigated, how it's done and how it's governed. This should sit within the organisation's wider governance framework and include appropriate processes, policies and procedures for assessing and approving all types of change to ensure that initiatives are within strategic, financial, operational, risk and technical appetites.

Without a framework to provide structure, standards and guiding principles, there won't be any consistency to how change is done. That said, the change framework shouldn't be a rigid, complicated and unwieldy thing but appropriate for the organisation and its ways of working – it should add value. It should be flexible and evolve to fit ways of doing change as they evolve over time, for instance, by adapting to more agile methods.

LET'S TALK ABOUT... CHANGE FRAMEWORKS

I've seen change frameworks where it's been mandated to adhere to criteria that were not relevant or fit-for-purpose. Rather than applying common sense and adapting the framework, unnecessary activities and documentation were enforced which ended up increasing the project duration, added no value and caused angst and frustration for all involved.

Why you need a change capability

Without a change capability, how does change get deployed back into the BAU operation? Who fully understands and is realistically going to coordinate the activity required across all the areas impacted? The answer is no one – it isn't likely to happen.

Take a look at Figure 11. Changes requested by Team A, once approved, will be made *by* Team A *for* Team A – the same with Team G. For Team A's change, there may be no awareness of the impact it will have on Teams C, D and H, Figure 12. Team A will be solely focused on doing its day job and only concerned with how that is affected.

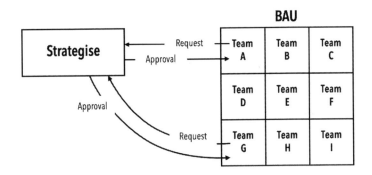

Figure 11: Without a change capability, changes requested by teams A and G are likely only to be implemented within those teams.

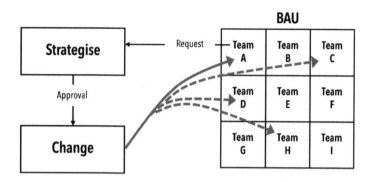

Figure 12: Change delivered with the impact across all areas considered.

Not having a change capability can easily result in a siloed and inefficient operation with fragmented and broken processes, lack of standards and lack of effective controls. There will be limited understanding of how the organisation as a whole operates – what's done, how it's done and who does it – along with poor communication and interaction between teams and functions. As well as incurring significantly higher than necessary operating costs, this also:

- Impedes the ability to grow the business, as people are working inefficiently so only have time to keep things going – they don't have the bandwidth to get involved with new revenue-generating or growth-related activities

- Impedes the ability to react swiftly to change as its impact won't be understood, so there is no business agility

- Increases the risk of operational failure, which could result in increased complaints, damage to reputation, data and regulatory breaches, and financial penalties

Operational resilience

Since Covid-19, there has been an increased focus on operational resilience – how effectively organisations deal with the consequences of unexpected and disruptive events.

In the UK, the financial services regulators, the Financial Conduct Authority (FCA) and Prudential Regulatory Authority (PRA) have mandated that firms operating in the financial services sector need to be able to prevent, adapt, respond to, recover and learn from operational disruption, with organisations having to identify their 'important business services'. These are their key processes that should remain operational (within defined tolerances) following a major unexpected event, so that the impact and any disruption to customers and the UK's financial system is minimised.

Whether industries are regulated or not, if an organisation does not fully understand how it operates, it will not be able to react to unforeseen changes swiftly or with confidence, to the possible detriment of both the organisation and its customers.

In the last chapter, we saw how the VUCA model was being increasingly applied to the business world. Without an effective change capability, organisations run the risk of not being able to react to unexpected events and unplanned change – there will be limited business agility and operational resilience.

LET'S TALK ABOUT... THE CONSEQUENCES OF NOT HAVING A CHANGE CAPABILITY

I previously worked with a company that had a near non-existent change capability, with business areas allowed to make changes as they wished with no governance or oversight. Unsurprisingly this caused regular problems. A couple of examples are outlined below, which in the first case resulted in remedial action to address the unforeseen consequences and, in the second, not being able to leverage the expected benefits.

- A seemingly minor and untested change made to the company's website inadvertently started stripping out documents that customers had attached to emails.

- A marketing campaign was launched promoting a particular product, but the business area that dealt with that product wasn't involved so were unable to deal with the resulting spike in demand.

These were the completely avoidable consequences of small changes being made without understanding the impact of change, or the appropriate testing and controls in place to identify and prevent such problems. Although the outcome in both cases was minor, there was still a negative impact on customers and the business, ie poor service provision with potential damage to reputation and increased operational costs (having to contact affected customers about the attachment issue), wasted cost and effort on the marketing campaign, and loss of additional revenue from not being able to meet the sudden increase in demand.

It's not hard to imagine how significant the consequences could be if more substantial changes were made.

Small change checklist

Of course, it isn't practical or possible to create a list that covers all the small changes that could be made across the business, and fortunately you don't need to. What you can do is identify some basic criteria that need to be satisfied for individual areas to make small changes without having to refer to the change team, for instance, by using a 'small change checklist'. For example, if the answer to the questions below is 'No', then the change could probably be made safely:

- Do customers see the output of the thing being changed?

- Do other teams or departments across the organisation use the thing being changed?

- Is this a new thing that doesn't currently exist?

- Is this the first time this type of change has been made?

- Does the change have to be made outside of working hours?

- Does the IT department need to be involved?

- Does the change need to be tested by other teams?

Any checklist would evolve over time, and in the early stages there may need to be regular conversations with the change team to refine the questions. But, even with referral to the change team, it would not automatically mean that a project has to be set up – there would simply be more confidence that the change could be made without any unforeseen consequences.

Using external expertise

Maybe you're an organisation that tends to rely on external parties such as consultancies or contractors when it comes to managing change and running most non-transformational projects and programmes? This may be the most appropriate way for you to resource these, but you should be conscious of not over-relying on them – you still need a change capability even if it's a basic one.

Why? Because any external party will not know your organisation as well as you do – or should do!

External parties will rely on what you tell them, and if you don't sufficiently understand how your BAU operation works, you won't get the results you expect.

As a minimum you should have some dedicated change resource, a basic change framework and a solid understanding of your current business and operating models. The current operating model, what it is and how to pragmatically define it, is discussed in the next three chapters.

For transformational change, though, even if you do have an internal change capability, you will likely need additional help and inevitably be working with multiple third parties.

Change capability and transformational change

Transformational change is disruptive. It moves the goalposts and redefines the playing field. It's not something that organisations do, or need to do, very often. Consequently, they are likely to have less experience of doing it, and as a result, it's easy to underestimate what's involved and misjudge how best to approach and execute it. And the consequences of getting it wrong can have huge implications, not only financially but on customer service, operating efficiency, regulatory compliance, reputation, and, ultimately, the potential viability of the organisation.

You may have a vision and a clear strategy for your organisation, but how do you get there from where you are currently? You will need to work with a variety of external parties along with a host of internal stakeholders to achieve this and, with the number of parties involved in transformation programmes, the effort required to understand and manage what they are all doing is much greater than that required for non-transformational change activities.

Along with the raft of internal stakeholders, you may have to deal with multiple solution providers, consultancies, system integrators, external subject matter experts, suppliers, organisations that you're integrating with, trade and regulatory bodies, etc.

Ensuring that every party knows and understands what it's doing can be a challenge. What I'm describing is just basic project management on steroids but, without being aware of this and knowing what could go wrong, you can easily lose control. Every party should be clear about its role in the programme and what it is accountable and responsible for doing.

LET'S TALK ABOUT... BROOKS'S LAW

Brooks's law[9] states that as the number of parties increases, the number of possible connections increases at an ever-faster rate. The more parties there are involved, the greater the management complexity and risk of miscommunication, misunderstanding and incorrect assumptions being made. To illustrate this:

- With 3 parties involved (A, B, C) there are 3 possible connections (A–B, A–C, B–C).
- Doubling the number of parties to 6 gives 15 possible connections.
- Quadrupling the number of parties to 12 gives 66 possible connections.

Take a look at Figure 13. The left side illustrates the activities being done by the organisation, represented by the black squares, with third-party activity represented by the light grey squares – everyone knows what they are doing. The right side illustrates what can happen if roles and responsibilities aren't clear. Activities can be missed, as represented by the white squares, where everyone thinks they are being done by another party, or activities are duplicated, represented by the dark grey squares.

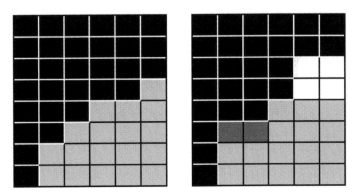

Figure 13: Clear roles and responsibilities (left), unclear roles and responsibilities (right) where activities are missed and duplicated.

The PMO function mentioned earlier should play a key role in supporting the transformation programme to ensure roles are clear. It may also be prudent, if it's warranted, to establish a dedicated transformation programme office for the duration of the programme.

There will be lot of touchpoints and therefore opportunities for things to go wrong. Knowing what every party is meant to be doing is one thing, but how do you know that all the parties you're working with are fully competent in what they do and how they do it? This is, after all, what your organisation will be paying for, but it may not always be the case.

For example, when dealing with solution providers, it's not uncommon for there to be a disconnect between their sales and delivery teams. The sales team may happily tell you, and may even have shown you in demonstrations, that their product can do A, B and C, but you may subsequently find out, once the sale has been concluded and contracts signed, that it can actually only do B, with A and C 'in development'.

When a solution provider says its product or service can do something, you must establish what they really mean. Does, 'Yes, it can' mean:

- It's fully developed, available and working with other customers using it right now in a live environment.

- It's developed but not actually being used anywhere yet.

- We can give you a demo but it hasn't been developed.

- It can be done, we just haven't done it yet – here are our thoughts about how it could work.

It's a bit like asking me if I can replace the engine in your car. I can… but I'd need to learn how to do it first and then get hold of the right equipment and tools. I'm pretty sure that I have the ability to do it – I've just never done it before and couldn't do it right now.

It's all about asking the right questions and knowing how to interpret the responses, which sounds obvious, but it's only obvious if you're aware of it.

Summary

If your organisation doesn't have a change capability you should seriously consider establishing one, and sooner rather than later. You should also look at your BAU operation to assess whether it's really operating as efficiently and effectively as you think it is. And, if you're embarking on a transformation programme, having an internal change capability and a good understanding of how your BAU operation works is essential.

We've now looked at what transformation means and who should do it, but what does it actually involve? In the next chapter, we'll look at the elements of the transformation journey, what they are and how they relate to one another.

Key points

- Without an effective change capability your organisation will not operate effectively or efficiently – there will be operational silos and broken processes, and you will be carrying an unnecessarily high level of risk.

- To have business agility and be operationally resilient, you need to understand the impact of change on your organisation.

- You should know your business better than any external party knows it.

- You will need external help for transformational change initiatives.

Food for thought

- Do you have an effective change capability – can you afford *not* to have one?

- Is there a fit-for-purpose change framework and is it adhered to?

- Do people feel as if change is done *with* them or done *to* them?

- Do you overly rely on external parties to provide change and project/programme expertise?

4
The Transformation Journey

In this chapter we:

- Look at the elements that make up the transformation journey and how they relate to one another

- Discuss business models and operating models in more detail and see why components can't be looked at in isolation

- See why it's so important to understand the current operating model

Scan the QR code to watch the accompanying video.

The point of any type of transformation is to bring about a step change in operation and performance and change the outcomes that your organisation achieves. This will inevitably require a shift in mindset, as well as possible changes to what your organisation does, but certainly changes to how it does it, defined by your business and operating models respectively.

Transformation is often, and rightly, described as a journey and as with any journey, there's a destination, a starting point, and a route to get you there.

Vision, mission and core values

The destination is encapsulated by the organisation's vision, which is a simple, high-level statement of where it wants to get to and what it ultimately wants to achieve – its purpose.

The organisation's mission statement describes, at a high level, how it intends to achieve its vision, and its core values are the beliefs, principles, and practices that guide the conduct of the organisation and the behaviour of its people in the pursuit of its vision.

Let's look at an example, IKEA. IKEA's vision, what it wants to achieve, is:

'To create a better everyday life for the many people'.[10]

Its mission, how it's going to do this, is to:

> 'Offer a wide range of well-designed, functional home furnishing products at prices so low that as many people as possible will be able to afford them'.

And IKEA has eight core values that underpin the organisation, shaping its culture and driving its behaviour:

- Togetherness – stronger together
- Caring for people and planet – make a significant and lasting impact
- Cost-consciousness – make more from less without compromising on quality
- Simplicity – staying close to reality
- Renew and improve – look for new and better ways going forward
- Different with a meaning – question existing solutions, think in unconventional ways, experiment and dare to make mistakes
- Give and take responsibility – empower people
- Lead by example – being our best self and bringing out the best in each other

Strategic goals

An organisation's vision and mission statements provide the ultimate heading, but it's the strategy that defines the goals and objectives that need to be achieved to realise its vision. These strategic goals will be shaped by the vision and influenced by multiple external factors, including:

- Regulation

- Competition

- Technology

- Customer needs and expectations

- ESG (environmental, social and governance) factors

- Economic, political and societal landscapes

The organisation's strategy may be supported by lower-level, divisional strategies (sales, marketing, claims, IT, etc) that should all align to the top-level strategy – they need to join up so that every part of the organisation is working towards common goals. The top-level strategy should be defined before the lower-level strategies – the tail should not wag the dog.

To fully achieve its strategic goals, the organisation needs to conduct its business – whatever that may be – and this is defined by its business model. Figure 14 illustrates how these elements are related.

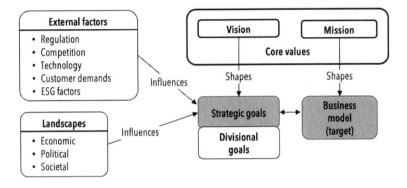

Figure 14: *The relationship between vision, mission, strategy, and an organisation's desired business model.*

Business models

The business model is a more detailed description of the mission statement and describes:

- What the organisation does – the products and services offered

- Who it does it for – its customers and markets

- How customers are served and how products and services are provided, sold, distributed and delivered – eg retail outlets, wholesale, online, franchise, partner models

In IKEA's case, that's designing, manufacturing and selling home furnishing products and services to its customers around the world, via stores, call centres and online channels. This is what IKEA exists to do and what it does to *create value* – this is what the business model describes.

Similarly, insurance companies exist to manage and transfer risk by providing and servicing insurance policies and managing and paying claims. Car manufacturers exist to sell and service vehicles, and charities exist to raise money and help causes.

Changing business model could mean anything from introducing a new distribution channel to radically changing what the organisation does. Over the past couple of decades many organisations have changed their business models by introducing a digital channel to offer products and services via the internet. Some well-known companies have more radically changed their business models, including:

- Microsoft – from selling operating systems and software to providing licensed software and cloud infrastructure, as well as actively partnering with other companies

- Netflix – originally providing DVD rentals to the public using the postal service, but now providing streamed content to internet-connected devices

- Amazon – having started as an online bookstore, it has morphed into an internet-based business enterprise providing e-commerce, cloud computing, digital streaming and AI services

The purpose of changing business models is to make a structural shift to the organisation to enable greater value to be created. This may include the more obvious goals of unlocking new avenues of revenue and profitability, but also creating opportunities to positively increase the organisation's impact on society and the environment.

But business models don't and can't exist on their own. Home furnishers, insurance companies, car manufacturers and charities don't exist to support IT systems, hire staff, produce annual accounts or buy ink for printers, but they need to do all these things and countless more to be able to execute their business models, and it's their operating models that enable and support this.

An organisation that wants to transform may not want or need to change its business model, but it will certainly want to change outcomes and how the business model is executed, and that means changing its operating model. This was the case with the transformation of the British Cycling team, which we looked at in Chapter Two. British Cycling didn't change what was done – it was still competitive cycling – but it transformed how it was done to achieve totally different outcomes, ie winning more medals and setting new records.

Operating models

There are two flavours of operating model to be aware of:

- Target operating model (TOM) – this describes the ideal, future operating state.

- Current operating model (COM) – this describes the current operating state, ie the BAU operation.

Target operating model (TOM)

In a perfect world, an organisation would be able to execute its business model... perfectly – with all its strategic objectives and goals fully achieved. To do this though, it would need to operate in a perfect state – and that state is described by the TOM.

But don't forget, the TOM is just that, a target, something to aim for. It will never actually be realised as the factors that shape and influence the strategic goals, and hence the business model and the TOM, will change quicker than your organisation can adapt to them. This is why you should review your TOM when strategy is reviewed, as both are intrinsically linked and need to stay aligned.

TOMs can also be produced at divisional or departmental levels. However, it's not unusual for these lower-level models to be constructed before a top-level TOM exists. As such, the lower-level models may be defined in relative isolation – in silos – so you end up with lots of TOMs created to different standards that don't fit together and don't fully support the business model. This is why you should create the top-level TOM first.

The components of the TOM are:

- Organisational design and structure
- Organisational culture, mindset and leadership styles
- People, roles, skills, development paths and working patterns
- Governance frameworks, corporate and operational appetites, communication and reporting
- Workflows, processes and journeys
- Data
- Applications and systems
- Networks and infrastructure

Current operating model (COM)

The starting point of any transformation journey is defined by the COM. Its components mirror those in the TOM but, as the name suggests, the COM describes how they work and interact with one another *now*. Organisations often have a poor understanding of their COM, and that can be problematic (as I'll illustrate later).

Change roadmap

The route between the starting and end points of the transformation journey, defined by the COM and TOM respectively, is set out in the organisation's change roadmap. This describes the strategic and tactical initiatives to be undertaken to move the current BAU operating state closer to its target state, and as we saw in the previous chapter, it's the organisation's change capability that delivers the projects and programmes required.

The relationship between all the elements of the transformation journey is shown in Figure 15.

The impact of transformational change

Transformational change may or may not significantly affect the organisation's business model, but it will certainly impact its operating model, with each

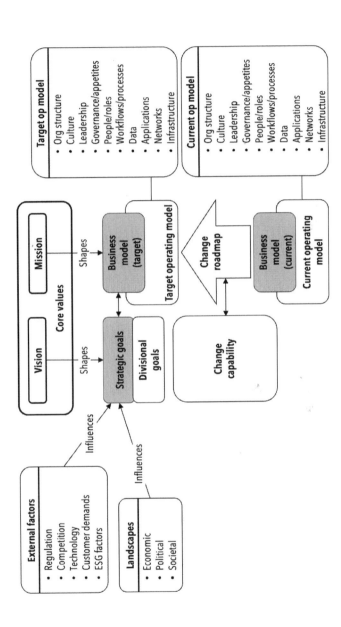

Figure 15: The relationship between the elements of the transformation journey.

of the COM's components affected to a greater or lesser degree. A key point to appreciate is that these components are all connected. You can't look at elements in isolation. They must be considered together, holistically, to understand the impact of change and to enable the effective management of that change. If your organisation isn't used to undertaking transformational change, you should be mindful of taking too siloed an approach.

Figure 16 shows a current business model and the components of the COM running along the bottom, with their target states at the top. Any transformation initiative will impact some or all these components, moving them from their current state closer to their target state, and in doing so satisfy some strategic objectives.

External expertise revisited

Figure 16 also illustrates the potential aspects of overreliance on third parties. For example, if you're implementing or replacing a core technology platform as an enabler for your organisation's transformation, you will be working with the vendor of that platform. Let's illustrate this using a fictitious vendor called 'No Idea Solutions' (NIS).

Now, NIS should know what their platform can do and how it could best be used by organisations like yours, but you shouldn't rely on this being the case.

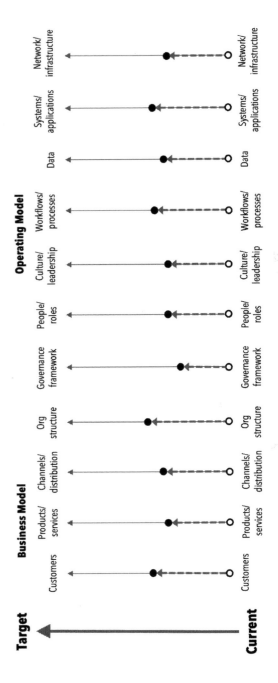

Figure 16: Transformational change impacts business and operating model components to differing degrees.

NIS's primary objective and focus will be on implementing their system, which may directly impact the workflows and processes, data, systems and applications, and network and infrastructure components of your operating model. How using their platform impacts components beyond these is unlikely to be top of NIS's priorities (and likely to be outside of their expertise), so do not rely on them to tell you how to, for example, restructure your organisation, reengineer your processes or improve your governance framework – the onus is on you to determine this.

NIS's priorities may also be at odds with your best interests. For example, NIS may be a bit too keen to push certain features and capabilities that you just don't need, in an attempt to generate additional licensing revenue, or add additional resources to work on the programme (regardless of whether they add any value to what's being done). It's important to remember what vendors are there to do, and be mindful of where their expertise lies, questioning anything that doesn't stack up. They will not have all the answers, despite what they may tell you.

An additional factor to be aware of when there are multiple external parties is whether they will all get along with one another and co-operate in a professional way (which you'd hope), or whether they may try to compete with each other and blame one another if things don't go to plan (which unfortunately is quite possible).

On the flip side, solution providers should be aware of possible risks to their reputation. Continuing with the example from above, NIS may have a limited view of its client's wider transformation programme and how well or not it's being run. The programme may involve significant changes to components outside of NIS's influence, or that NIS has limited sight of. If the programme goes awry or fails, regardless of how successful the technical implementation of the platform may have been, the technology – and hence NIS – may have blame unfairly apportioned to them. It's always easy to blame technology.

Ideally, solution providers should have some awareness of the overall transformation programme objectives and how the programme is being run as, without this, their reputation and that of their product, are (at least in part) at the mercy of the organisation's change capability – good, bad or ugly.

It's all connected

Every aspect of the transformation journey is connected, from the vision, strategy and target business and operating models to all the components of the current operating model. It is not possible to look at elements in isolation without introducing unnecessary risk. Each component shapes or supports the others, as seen in Figure 17.

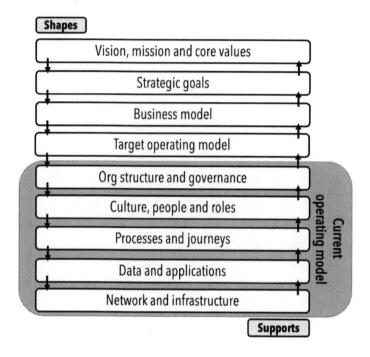

Figure 17: It's all connected.

The importance of the current operating model

Understanding your organisation's COM is a very important part of any transformation initiative. To illustrate why, let's consider an actual journey. Figure 18 shows a map of Britain, and you want to go to Scotland (ringed).

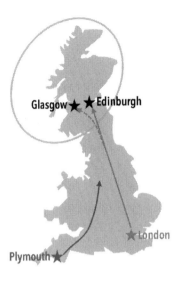

Figure 18: The importance of understanding your COM.

If you start from London and head for Edinburgh, you may initially plan the light grey route, although you may receive some new information en route and decide to go to Glasgow instead. As long as you're clear about the overall objective, ie being in Scotland, the specific destination is not critically important to your initial heading, and you can change direction with minimal impact, illustrated by the dotted grey line.

But if you don't sufficiently understand the starting point, perhaps setting off from Plymouth instead, this gives a very different route, and in programme terms, a different plan. The approach, direction and priorities may be wrong, with focus on the wrong things and incorrect assumptions made. A quote from the organisational theorist Kenichi Ohmae puts this nicely:

'Rowing harder doesn't help if the boat is headed in the wrong direction.'[11]

Having a comprehensive understanding of your COM is fundamental to successful transformation and also provides you with a valuable, reusable and maintainable corporate asset – a single source of operational truth. With this, you'll understand the impact of change, negate the need for projects and programmes to determine the 'as-is' from scratch every time, and provide the solid underpinnings of a genuinely agile and resilient operation.

Summary

Business models and operating models are concepts that apply to all organisations regardless of size. Some (probably smaller) organisations may be unaware of them, but they are there, and it's important to have an awareness and understanding of them as they provide a foundation and frame of reference for change. This particularly applies to transformational change as its impact is so wide reaching.

The significance of understanding the organisation's COM is often not fully appreciated, although if it is, there is sometimes too much focus on process and it can quickly become too detailed to be usable and maintainable. In the next chapter, we'll look at how to practically define and construct the COM.

Key points

- Transformation may not involve significant changes to the organisation's business model, but it will always involve changes to outcomes, mindsets and the operating model.

- Business and operating model components are all connected – they can't be looked at in isolation – a holistic approach is vital.

- Understanding the current operating model provides a foundation for transformation and a valuable corporate asset.

- Solution providers and consultancies may not always act in your best interests and their priorities may not always be the same as yours – success is far more likely when they are aligned to yours.

Food for thought

- Do you have defined vision and mission statements?

- Would colleagues know what your organisation's values are?

- Do you have clearly defined current business and operating models?

- How often do you review strategy (and do you review your TOM at the same time)?

5
The Current Operating Model

In this chapter we:

- Look at 'process' and see why it can be tricky to define

- Define the key ingredients required to construct a basic COM

- See why a holistic, cross-functional view is so important

Scan the QR code to watch the accompanying video.

There aren't any good reasons for organisations not to know how they operate, but many don't have a good view of this. There needs to be an understanding of how the whole operation hangs together – a cross-functional and holistic view that is available and visible to everyone across the organisation, and doesn't only exist in people's heads. It's the COM that describes this, though what this involves is often poorly understood.

Understanding the COM means that when you want to change something, be it a relatively small process improvement exercise or something more transformational, you will know the areas of the organisation that are impacted and, at a high level, how. You won't necessarily know at the outset – and don't need to know – the detail of the impact of change, but you will have a good idea of the scale of change and who needs to be engaged to understand that detail.

So what's the alternative to not knowing?

If you don't understand your COM, once you have decided what you want to achieve from your initiative, be it big or small, you'll have to undertake an exercise to find out which areas will be impacted. If the change is small, that may be easy, although as mentioned in Chapter Three, there can often be unforeseen consequences to seemingly harmless changes. If the change is transformational though, this may be a lengthy exercise and one that can easily see areas overlooked. Do you really want or need that risk?

As we also saw in Chapter Three, as a result of the Covid-19 pandemic, operational resilience is a higher priority on boards' agendas than it was previously. Being operationally resilient is directly linked with being able to react to planned and unplanned change swiftly, confidently and with minimal risk – that's having *business agility*.

But organisations can easily get bogged down in detail when trying to do this by focusing too much on process.

LET'S TALK ABOUT... TOO MUCH PROCESS

A company that had been defining its operating model for over a year asked me to review what they were doing as they didn't feel they were making as much progress as they had expected. It quickly became apparent that what they'd been doing was documenting customer journeys and mapping processes, and to a very detailed degree. The body of work that had been produced was quite substantial, though much of it was of little value as it was too detailed to be realistically maintainable, and no attention had been given to the non-process components of the operating model. The approach was revised and effort refocused, although at the expense of many wasted months.

Setting the scene

Before we look at how to construct a basic COM, there are some ways of thinking and principles that need to be clarified.

What is process?

The problem with talking about process* is that it can be used in many ways, at different levels, and involves multiple factors.

Google's English dictionary (provided by Oxford Languages) defines the noun 'process' as:

> 'A series of actions or steps taken in order to achieve a particular end'.[12]

I'm going to define this slightly differently – a process is:

> 'A series of functions performed in a defined sequence by an entity/entities to achieve an agreed outcome',
>
> where:

- 'Function' is the activity or set of activities performed, ie *what* is done

---

* I'm talking about all types of process including customer journeys etc.

- 'Entity' is the thing that performs the function, eg departments, teams or systems, as well as external parties (including customers), ie *who* (or *what*) performs the function

- 'Outcome' is the objective of the function, ie *why* it's being done

Regarding entities, there's an important distinction to be aware of between 'the thing performing a function' and 'what's used to perform a function'. This is particularly relevant when considering something that's done by a person versus automated activity. For example, telephoning a contact centre to buy something involves interacting with a person, whereas buying online doesn't – you're interacting with a system. But for the purposes of defining the COM, it's the entity *performing the function* that needs to be considered, ie the person in the contact centre, and the system for the online sale, Table 2.

Table 2: For defining the COM, it's the entity performing the function that needs to be considered

Channel	Entity performing the function	Used to perform the function
Telephone	Contact centre (person)	System
Online	System	System

My revised definition of process addresses *what* is done, *who* does it and *why*, but in addition to these three factors, 'process' can also describe *how*, *when* and *where* something is done. Talking about process can be complicated and it helps to have a consistent and common language to prevent confusion, ie an agreed terminology, but keep it simple and make it intuitive and sensible so that everyone knows what you mean when you're talking about process.

Purpose of the COM – the source of operational truth

The primary purpose of the COM is to describe the organisation's current operating state, what the various components involved are, how they work, and how they interact with one another – it is a source of *operational truth*. As we saw in the previous chapter, the components are:

- Organisational design and structure

- Organisational culture, mindset and leadership styles

- People, roles, skills, development paths and working patterns

- Governance frameworks, corporate and operational appetites, communication and reporting

- Workflows, processes and journeys

- Data

- Applications and systems

- Networks and infrastructure

You can easily see that focusing on process is going to be limiting as it's just one of the many factors that need to be considered to have a complete view.

Entities and functions – finding the right level

When defining the COM, it's important to determine the appropriate level to work at. The level of granularity required will depend on the nature of the organisation and its complexity.

An organisation consists of entities representing differing levels of granularity, ie divisions, departments, teams, etc, and each of these entities performs a key function. Table 3 illustrates an HR department that performs the HR function and, at a lower level of granularity, the HR teams – recruitment, payroll and benefits – and the functions they perform.

The functions each team performs may then be further broken down into sub-functions. For example, the recruitment function may comprise of sourcing, screening and onboarding sub-functions.

Table 3: Determining the appropriate level of entities and functions is an important first step when creating the COM

Dept	Dept function	Team	Team function	Team sub-function
HR	Provides HR services	Recruitment	Manages all permanent and temporary recruitment	Sourcing
				Screening
				Onboarding
		Payroll	Manages and administers payroll services for permanent and temporary resources	Payroll team's sub-functions
		Benefits	Administers all employee benefits	Benefits team's sub-functions

More information – detail or context?

Detail is important and, of course, it's crucial to understand the detail of any situation to obtain the best outcome. By skipping over the detail, you run the risk of missing or fundamentally misunderstanding something of critical importance. That said, you need to know when to care about the detail and when not to, as being too detailed at the wrong time can impede progress and add minimal value. You need to recognise when it's not important and not material to the situation at hand so you can focus on what is needed.

An analogy... it's raining and you need to get a taxi, so you call a taxi firm or use an app to book one. You don't need to have a conversation or enter details about the make of car, whether it has an automatic gearbox or not, or specify its colour. These are details that you don't need to care about. Knowing these adds no value to your objective of getting to the station without getting wet.

You do, of course, need to have confidence that basic expectations are going to be met. If there is any doubt, regardless of how obvious it may seem, there is never any harm in confirming the seemingly obvious to eliminate ambiguity and establish clarity. You wouldn't really want the taxi in Figure 19 turning up, would you?

Figure 19: Probably not the taxi you were expecting.[13]

When defining the COM, if the amount of information being generated starts to become unmanageable, consider the consequences of *not* knowing the detail – is it really required at this stage?

But it's not just providing unnecessary detail that can cause problems.

Another analogy... imagine you're lost in a forest but fortunately have a radio to communicate with your would-be rescuers. They ask you to describe your surroundings and you tell them that you're standing 1.65 metres from a tree that's 9.5 metres tall. You have indeed provided more information, but you've given *detail* when you really need to give *context*. For example, that you're by a stream at the edge of a clearing about 100 metres from a cliff face.

Context is essential to establish clarity and understand the bigger picture and how things fit together. It also helps people to understand what needs to be done, what's required of them and why. To further illustrate this, Figure 20 shows a partially completed jigsaw. If you were asked to identify the painting (your objective), despite not having all the pieces (the detail), you can clearly see it's the Mona Lisa.

In the next sections I'll describe some simple techniques to create a basic COM.

Figure 20: Despite only being partially completed,
this is clearly the Mona Lisa.[14]

Key ingredients

Operating models are complex. Describing the components involved and how they work together to explain in a logical, digestible and pragmatic way how an organisation operates can seem daunting. However, sticking to my preferred approach to everything,

I like to apply the KISS principle and keep things as simple as possible.[15]

While there are specific applications and tools available to help create operating models and capture and manage the knowledge that exists within organisations, for many, the COM can be simply defined using common tools, eg spreadsheets and basic flow-charting software.

Regardless of the tools used it's always good to understand why you're doing something, rather than just blindly doing it, and the techniques below provide that understanding. There are only three ingredients required to define a basic COM:

- The entities that exist within an organisation
- The function(s) that each entity performs
- The end-to-end processes an organisation employs to deliver its business model

Entities

First, list all the entities that exist within your organisation, and the third parties it deals with, to an appropriate level of granularity. Table 4 illustrates this using an insurance company as an example. An organisational structure chart, system or application inventory and supplier list should help with this.

Table 4: A list of the organisation's entities

Division	Department	Team
General Insurance	New Business	Contact centre
		Underwriting
		Online support
		Back-office administration
	Claims	Triage
		Claim management
		Settlement
Central Services	HR	Recruitment
		Payroll
		Benefits

Functions

Next, for each of the entities, add a short description of the functions performed. To illustrate this, Table 5 describes the high-level functions performed by the four teams that make up the New Business department.

Table 5: The functions that the entities perform

Entity			Function
Division	Department	Team	
General Insurance	New Business	Contact centre	Provides quotations and sells policies directly to customers via telephony channels

Continued

Table 5: The functions that the entities perform (cont).

Entity			Function
Division	Depart-ment	Team	
		Underwriting	For non-standard requests, assesses risks and decides whether to quote and how much to charge
		Online support	Deals with customer queries that come in via digital channels
		Back-office administration	Provides all non-customer-facing new business administration activities

Primary end-to-end processes

Last, list the primary end-to-end processes that the organisation uses to execute its business model. Continuing with the above example, an insurance company provides and services insurance policies and manages and pays claims, and its primary end-to-end processes include:

- New business – providing insurance quotations and selling policies

- Servicing – making changes to a customer's insurance policy as needs change, eg moving house, changing car

- Renewal – renewing a policy at the end of each year so that insurance cover continues

- Claims – managing and paying claims covered by the insurance policy

Each of these primary processes will contain several high-level functions, which should be listed. Table 6 shows the headline functions performed for the end-to-end new business process.

Table 6: List of functions involved in the end-to-end new business process

Primary process	Functions involved	Function description
New business	Onboard customers	Establish eligibility and create the client record
	Quote	Capture risk information and provide a quotation
	Buy	Take payment for the policy
	Issue documents	Issue documentation for the purchased policy
	Allocate payments	Allocate money received to the policy

Of course, organisations perform many more processes than those involved in their primary business activity, and all processes could eventually be included, but start with the primary processes.

Constructing the COM

After carrying out the actions above, you have two lists:

- An exhaustive list of entities with a simple description of the functions performed by each one

- A list of the primary end-to-end processes and the associated sequence of functions involved

As well as being easy to understand, the information provided by these lists is also relatively static – it is not subject to constant change so can be easily maintained and kept up to date. You can now create specific views.

Entity interactions

The first view to create involves identifying the direct touchpoints between entities involved in the BAU operation. These entity interactions can be represented as diagrams or tables and are process agnostic, ie you are establishing which entities directly interact with one another in the day-to-day operation of the business regardless of the reason. It is easier to do this initially by working at the department level, otherwise it can quickly become overcomplicated. The exercise can be subsequently repeated to consider team-level interactions, if this adds value.

Continuing our example from above, all the different entities that have a direct touchpoint with the New Business department should be listed – internal departments, external third parties and customers – with the headline reason for each interaction noted. Table 7 shows an example of an entity interaction table.

Table 7: The entities with direct touchpoints to the New Business department

Entity	Direct touchpoint	Internal / external	Interaction reason
New Business department	Customer	External	Request for quotation
	Other insurers	External	Requests for information
	Credit agencies	External	Credit checks for finance (if required)
	Payment providers	External	Companies offering payment methods
	Brokers	External	Request for quotation acting on behalf of customers
	Claims	Internal	Previous claims information
	Finance	Internal	Setting up bespoke payment terms
	Complaints	Internal	Registering a complaint
	IT	Internal	Technical support
	HR	Internal	Recruitment support

By repeating this exercise for all departments, you will know which ones may be impacted when changes need to be made in any one of them. Again, this is not a view that should change frequently, so the maintenance overhead is low.

Workflows

Workflows describe how work moves (flows) through an organisation. They are not process maps as they are only concerned with *what* functions are performed, the entities that perform them, and why work is routed to each entity.

To construct workflow views I use a simple technique I call POET analysis – point-of-existence to point-of-expiry. This simply asks, for a specific end-to-end process, what entities (teams or systems) touch the work as it moves through the organisation, and what the criteria are – the business rules or routing rules – that determine why it is routed to a particular entity?

This starts from the trigger event – the action that caused the work to come into existence – and finishes at the expiry of the work, ie when no further activity is required. This is best done initially for the primary end-to-end processes and by focusing on the 'happy path' for each process, ie ignoring exception routes.

This is represented by the thick arrow in Figure 21. Once the happy path is defined, entities involved in any exception processing can be incorporated and the business rules noted.

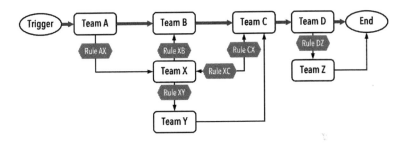

Figure 21: Workflows show what entities are involved in doing work and why work is routed to them.

There is one further thing to be aware of with workflows, and that relates to the 'flow' aspect. Looking at Figure 22, once the activities in Function 1 have been completed, the work can then move to Function 2 so those activities can be performed. There are two components involved in the move between Functions 1 and 2:

- Transfer time – the time taken from the completion of Function 1 to when Function 2 activity could start

- Queue time – the time from when Function 2 activity could start to when it actually starts

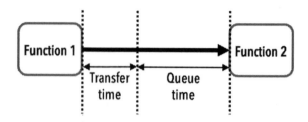

Figure 22: Transfer time and queue time.

Entity interaction diagrams and workflows are entity-focused views. The next stages incorporate the functions performed.

Entity-function matrices

Entity-function matrices are a simple way of representing the functions performed by teams. They also provide a way of identifying where similar types of work are done and can indicate where there are potential areas of duplication and where functions could be removed, consolidated or rationalised.

Table 8 shows that Teams A and C from Department X both perform an enquiry function (Function 4), as do Teams B and C in Department Y. If there isn't an overarching view of the BAU operation, opportunities to consolidate the enquiry function, or at least question if there's merit in consolidating it, may not be spotted.

Table 8: Entity-function diagrams show the functions performed by team-level entities

Function	Department X			Department Y		
	Team A	Team B	Team C	Team A	Team B	Team C
Function 1	X					
Function 2	X					
Function 3		X	X			
Function 4 – enquiries	X		X		X	X
Function 5				X		
Function 6						X

Entity-function interactions

Entity-function interaction diagrams build on the workflow diagrams. They show the relationships between entities for specific processes, and by adding the functions that are performed by each entity, a functional flow is produced. Figure 23 shows the new business process from earlier.

The functional flow gives a view of the end-to-end process through an organisational (entity and workflow) lens rather than a more complicated and detailed process lens. What this doesn't give is a view of how each of the functions breaks down into its processes and tasks, ie the detailed process flow. This is perfectly fine, as knowing the detail is *not* the point of defining the COM.

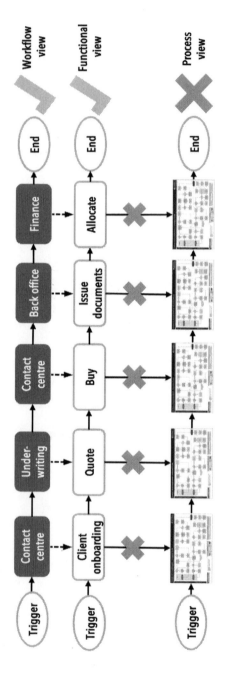

Figure 23: Entity-function interactions are an extension of workflow diagrams.

Inputs and outputs

The final step is to add each function's inputs and outputs to the entity-function interaction diagrams. Each function in an end-to-end process will have a defined set of inputs (key information and things needed to perform the function) and outputs (the results of completing each function). Inputs and outputs may include products in various stages of completion, sets of information, correspondence, authorisations, etc.

By defining the functional flow and the inputs and outputs, a complete description of the end-to-end process can be produced with absolute confidence that it hangs together with no breaks or disconnects. It's not of any interest at this stage what happens within functions or how efficiently they are performed, only what happens at the functions' boundaries, Figure 24.

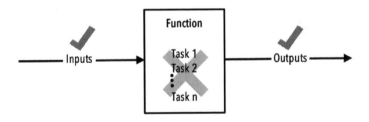

Figure 24: Inputs and outputs need to be known,
but not the activity within functions.

You now have a basic but comprehensive and maintainable view of your BAU operation.

Layering

Because of the relative simplicity of this construct, it's easy to apply different lenses to build up a more complete description of the COM, eg applications used, information flows, finance flows. Each layer gives a different perspective, and the combination of these layers allows increased understanding of the COM. Further, by extending the COM to include interactions with external parties, the ecosystem that the organisation operates in can also be defined.

A holistic approach

Imagine ten people who'd never seen a mug. If they were each shown one of the images in Figure 25 and asked to describe what they saw, they wouldn't necessarily realise that they were all looking at the same thing. Different perspectives are needed to get a complete and accurate understanding of the whole, so non-conformist views shouldn't immediately be dismissed if they don't initially align with the majority – they may be perfectly valid.

Figure 25: One mug, multiple perspectives.[16]

A cross-functional and holistic view also benefits process improvement initiatives. If you wanted to improve the end-to-end process in Figure 26, by looking at each of the five functions in isolation, you may be able to obtain an efficiency gain of 10% in each function – an overall improvement of 10% (assuming each carried equal weight). But improving each step does not necessarily mean that the process as a whole is optimised to its full extent. Looking holistically across the end-to-end process may reveal that by increasing the time spent in Function 2 by 10%, the time needed in Function 3 is reduced by 20% and by 40% in Functions 4 and 5 – an overall improvement of 20%. This may not be realised if a siloed approach is taken.

Figure 26: An increase in time spent in one function may result in an overall saving.

It's also important to look at the workflow aspects to see whether changes could be made to reduce transfer and queue times.

Summary

Constructing a basic COM only requires knowledge of an organisation's structure and what the entities do. It sounds simple but if it's approached in the wrong way, it can become incredibly complicated, and ultimately provide little or no value.

It's important not to get hung up on defining the detail and trying to incorporate everything at once. You need to have different views, different perspectives and build up layers of understanding, which is why it's imperative to focus effort at the right level.

Key points

- 'Process' is a multifaceted term encapsulating what, who, why, when, where and how something is done – be as clear as possible when talking about it.

- The current operating model provides the source of operational truth.

- When more information is required, consider whether it's detail or context that's needed.

- Think workflow, not process.

- KISS! Keep it simple – create a basic COM and then introduce different perspectives to add layers of information.

Food for thought

- Have you defined your COM and, if so, does it focus too much on process?

- Does anyone in your organisation really have a cross-functional view of the BAU operation?

- Are you aware of silos within your organisation and the extent to which they inhibit performance and operational efficiency?

6
Further Operating Model Considerations

In this chapter we:

- Look at the impact of a negative culture

- Highlight a further consequence of not understanding the COM

- See how COMs and ecosystems are fragmenting and becoming more complex

- Look at the TOM

- Discuss how to minimise reluctance and resistance to change

So far, we have largely focused on the organisational and workflow related aspects needed to create a basic COM. But there are some important points to be aware of relating to the other components, particularly governance and culture, as well as factors to consider when creating TOMs and defining new ways of working.

Culture and success

An organisation's culture is key in determining how successfully it can run its BAU operation and instigate, manage and deliver change. Any form of governance, be it corporate, operational, or project, etc, can only be effective if the right culture exists – one that doesn't rely on fear or persecuting people, but promotes values of integrity, fairness and transparency, and is open and ethical, where people take responsibility and are accountable for their actions. Essential for good governance is having the right information available at the right time to allow informed decisions to be made.

Making informed decisions

Organisations should be drowning in data. There is certainly enough of it out there, and the volume of data is only going to increase as technology continues to advance. With more and more data available, organisations should be able to better understand their customers, improve operational performance, reduce costs, design better products and enhance their services. But data on its own is almost useless.

Just because you may have access to lots of data, it doesn't mean you're using it in a productive way and making good decisions. You need to know what to do with the data and how to use it. To do that, you need to understand what you want to achieve – what it is you want to find out, what questions you want answered, what problems you're trying to solve, what issues you want to address, and what opportunities you want to exploit. This means having a clear vision and direction for your organisation and a comprehensive understanding of your current operation, defined by the COM.

With this understanding, you can then define the information you need, and hence what data is required. And with better information, you are more likely to make better informed decisions. Having accurate and credible information reduces the risk of making the wrong decisions, focusing on the wrong things, and heading in the wrong direction. Without sufficient or accurate information, you're as good as guessing.

But even with accurate information, if the culture within the organisation isn't one that welcomes and encourages transparency, how do you know that the necessary information is getting to the right people at the right time?

Message dilution

With the right culture, leaders and leadership teams will be receptive to accurate information regardless of whether the news it brings is good, bad or ugly.

Any organisation with a negative, toxic culture where bad news isn't tolerated, and only good news is 'allowed' is not going to operate effectively. Its leaders will never be aware of the reality of the BAU operation or the true status of projects and programmes. They will never be in receipt of the accurate information needed to make the right decisions to improve things – they will be out of touch and disconnected from reality.

Figure 27 illustrates how messages can become diluted as they move up the management chain. Significant problems and issues may exist at the coalface of the operation but if the culture isn't open, messages may become diluted so that at the executive level, where action could be taken to address issues, they have been so diluted no action is deemed necessary.

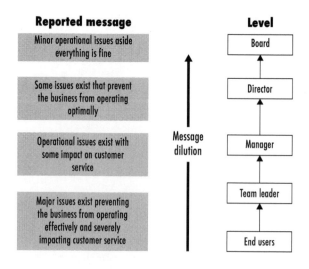

Figure 27: A toxic culture can dilute messages as they move up the management chain.

Remediating a misunderstood COM

I have emphasised the importance of the organisation's COM, and the consequences of embarking on a transformation initiative if it's not sufficiently understood, but there is a further aspect to note. Figure 28 illustrates a transformation journey with an incorrectly understood start point (COM*) and a correct one (COM). If starting from the incorrect point, at some stage during the execution of the programme (point A), it will be realised that the direction is wrong.

Not only will it take time, effort and cost to work out what needs to be done to recover the programme and get it back on track, ie changing direction and moving to point B, but work already done will need to be reviewed to ensure it is still valid, as denoted by the crosshatched area. The later it's realised that the COM wasn't sufficiently understood, the more rework there is likely to be.

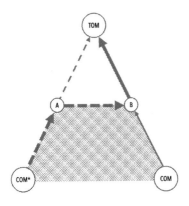

Figure 28: Consequences of not understanding your COM.

Alternatively, you may decide to live with some of the consequences of work already done. This could include increasing *technical debt*, where shortcuts are taken to make immediate technical development easier, but at the expense of efficiency in the longer term, for example, by hard coding instead of developing something that's configurable. *Operational debt* could also be increased with compromises made to the business operation, such as introducing convoluted processes or even manual workarounds.

Any compromises made will impact the benefits case and over time lead to an increasingly clunky and inefficient operation that gets harder and more costly to manage, support and change.

Fragmenting operating models and ecosystems

As technology has advanced, organisations are doing less and less themselves and are increasingly using third parties to provide services and products more cost effectively (at least in theory). Gone are the days when an organisation did everything in-house and administered its business on a small number of monolithic systems. The COM, which was once relatively simple (represented by the top image in Figure 29) is now far more complex, Figure 29 (bottom), and it's continuing to fragment as technology and the use of third parties increases. The line between an organisation's COM and the ecosystem it operates in is also blurring – the ecosystem being an extension of the COM that incorporates the external entities involved in the BAU operation, including:

- Third parties that perform functions that have been outsourced

- Third-party information sources that enrich or provide additional data, eg social media, government, regulatory and industry bodies, as well as IoT (Internet of things) devices and sensors that provide real-time information

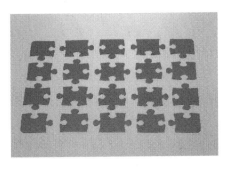

*Figure 29: Once simple operating models (top)[17]
are fragmenting as operating environments become
more complex (bottom).[18]*

Operational complexity is much greater than it used to be and it's more important than ever to understand how it all fits together.

The target operating model

Defining how things could be done and how the organisation may look in the future can be difficult given the number of components to consider. It's not just a case of overlaying a technology solution on top of reengineered processes. It's a collaborative and iterative exercise that needs input from all sides to understand the art of the possible, and consequently determine how the components of the operating model can best work together to achieve the organisation's strategic goals.

People

Effectively communicating change so people understand what's being done and why isn't enough. The impact that the change will have on the organisation's people needs to be understood, and they have to be appropriately supported through that change. This is particularly the case with transformational change, where roles are very likely to be impacted.

Existing knowledge and skills across the organisation should be assessed and compared to those that are going to be required, with gaps identified and action taken to close them. People need to be supported throughout the transformation process to help them adapt to new ways of working, with training provided to help them develop existing skills and learn new ones.

And of course, people have to be engaged *before* any change happens. Change should be done *with* them, not *to* them.

Perceptions and assumptions

If you're thinking about embarking on a transformation initiative, you'll hear lots of views, wanted or not, on what must or mustn't, should or shouldn't, can or can't be done. Some of these will be valid – some will just be noise.

There will be a lot of assumptions that have to be made at the outset. There is no escaping this. You may have a clear understanding of the outcomes and goals you want to achieve, and the direction needed, but the journey won't be fully known – there will be dragons! Establish as much clarity and certainty as possible and be explicit in requests and explanations to eliminate ambiguity, but recognise that there will be areas where this is not possible. In these cases you need to acknowledge and embrace the uncertainty, while seeking to eliminate it at the earliest opportunity. This will be an ongoing process throughout the duration of the programme and you should frequently review, validate or disprove your assumptions, and update plans accordingly.

Do not take things at face value, and state the obvious if you think it needs stating. Always question and challenge to ensure everyone has the correct understanding. All parties must be on the same page – something is only obvious if everyone knows it. If there's any doubt, even slight, then state it. It could end up saving a lot of time and money.

Future operating principles

When creating a new TOM and devising new ways of working, you should define and agree key operating principles before doing any organisational or process redesign. These don't have to be complex or detailed, just principles and guidelines that reflect what you're doing and support the outcomes you're trying to achieve.

Operating principles are not set in stone, so they can be violated, but there should be justifiable reasons for not adhering to them. Some examples of operating principles include:

- Capture data once and at the first opportunity.

- Capture data in a structured way so it can be easily reused in downstream processes and for reporting – unstructured data, such as free format text, is harder to use.

- Maximise peoples' time – people are employed to do particular jobs so maximise their value by removing administration and low-value-adding tasks as much as sensibly possible.

- Automate low-value-adding tasks.

- Minimise handoffs – these should only be made if value can be genuinely added or if value is destroyed by not doing so. If one person can do and complete a task, then one person should do it.

Having operating principles defined and agreed can prevent unnecessary debate and argument during subsequent phases of the programme.

Reluctance and resistance to change

People react to change in different ways. There will be some who are overly eager, and some who are reluctant and resistant. Tempering enthusiasm is easier to manage than overcoming resistance, but in all cases there is one simple thing that can be done to make everyone's life easier – communicate effectively.

Clearly stating the case for transformation, articulating why it's needed, the outcomes you want to achieve and setting expectations about what's going to be involved are essential. The level of detail you provide needs to differ depending on the audience, so teams that will be impacted by the change should be provided with more information than those that won't. However, there should always be mechanisms in place to enable people to find out more information, to ask questions and provide feedback, including doing so anonymously. There must also be frequent, simple and clear messaging about the transformation initiative from the programme and leadership teams.

Reluctance or resistance to change can arise from a range of factors, including:

- Concerns over job security and status

- Fear, reluctance to learn new things

- Change fatigue, disillusionment with previous failed initiatives

- Feeling ignored, lack of empathy, not being involved

- Stubbornness, bloody-mindedness

With effective communication, raising awareness and educating people, and being as open and transparent as possible, most of the above factors can be significantly mitigated. For example, if there is no risk or intention of job losses then say so – it will allay fears, stop rumours starting and allow people to focus on the things that you do want them to know.

When reluctance and resistance to change is obvious, it can be managed, but it's harder to identify passive-aggressive resistors – the people who will happily nod along and seemingly agree but then quietly (or perhaps not so quietly) cause disruption and angst when out of the spotlight. This behaviour can be subtle and easily deniable, 'Oh, I didn't realise it would be taken like that', 'Of course I didn't mean it that way', etc.

Identifying passive-aggressors can be difficult but you can detect them, and enhance your ability to manage any potential disruption, by fostering a positive programme environment. Along with clarity, effective communication and transparency, this involves engaging with key stakeholders early, getting them onside so they don't feel ignored or alienated.

Process decomposition

When defining new ways of working and new processes and journeys, there may be some people who are just bloody-minded and adamant that they won't change. They are irrationally entrenched in their position from the outset. This is genuine resistance rather than reluctance.

As we have discussed, one of the problems with defining new ways of working and new processes is that 'process' encompasses multiple questions: what, who, why, when, where and how. One way of dealing with people who are resistant to change is to focus on each of these aspects at a time and agree the purely objective, non-contentious ones first.

With any end-to-end process there will be an overall objective – why it is being done. This is the first thing to agree as there should be no argument with this. Similarly, the sequence of key functions involved in the end-to-end process should be able to be agreed with minimal issue. There is no discussion needed at this stage about *who* does the process, *when*, *where* or *how* it gets done. Once the sequence of functions is defined, we have an agreed end-to-end workflow. Each function will require certain inputs to enable it to be performed, and there will be specific outputs from the completion of each function. These should also be definable without any contention.

This still leaves where, when, who and how to be determined, but the scope and size of the issues left to discuss are a lot smaller as you've already agreed the objective aspects. You have a firm, non-arguable base to work from and can better understand what the remaining objections may be – if any. If the resistance turns out to be sheer bloody-mindedness, and there's an absolute unwillingness to get on board with the changes being proposed, the HR performance management route is always available.

Summary

A good culture underpins good governance and the ability for organisations to be sustainably successful. The more dysfunctional and toxic the culture is, the greater the risks the organisation will carry on multiple fronts – operational, regulatory, financial, commercial, reputational – as well as higher operating costs from unnecessary operating friction, staff turn-over and poor decision making.

Transformation is a journey, and you need to bring people with you, but given the complexities associated with transformational change, is it any wonder that many initiatives fail to deliver the results initially expected? And if you believe the often quoted '70% of transformation programmes fail' line, why on earth would you decide to embark on one in the first place?

In the next chapter, we'll look at how much credence this 70% failure figure really deserves.

Key points

- A good culture enables organisations to operate effectively and efficiently, and to manage risk and change successfully.

- Organisations need accurate data to provide meaningful information and to make informed decisions.

- Operating models are fragmenting so you need to understand how all the components fit together.

Food for thought

- Does your organisation make the best use of its data?

- How freely does information flow through your organisation – is it genuinely two-way?

- Can bad news be given and received without fear of blame or reprisal?

7

The Transformation Failure Myth

In this chapter we:

- Look at the origins of the often-cited 70% failure rate of transformation programmes

- Consider why this 70% figure continues to be used despite not being true

You may have heard or read that transformation programmes don't have a great chance of success, with a 70% failure rate often quoted. There have been many reports and articles that have referenced this 70% figure over the years, including those from the likes of McKinsey,[19] Boston Consulting Group,[20] PwC[21] and Deloitte.[22]

Believing your transformation initiative only has a 30% chance of succeeding is a rather scary prospect, and it begs the question of why any organisation would embark on such a programme when the odds of success are that low. Fortunately, there's no need to be fearful as it's simply untrue – much like the unicorn in Figure 30, it's a myth.

Figure 30: Both mythical – unicorns and the 70% failure rate of transformation programmes.[23]

Defining failure

Let's start by asking, 'what is the definition of failure here?' The claim is meaningless without understanding the criteria being applied. Are we talking about an absolute failure, and what does that mean? Is it financial collapse? Is it having to write off significant sums of time and money?

If failure means 'not fully achieving the expected benefits' then this relies on the expectations, assumptions and benefits being realistic in the first place.

As organisations sometimes have limited experience of transformational change, it's not hard to imagine that initial expectations may be unrealistic due to the lack of understanding of what's involved, the complexities and challenges that can arise, and the impact on all parts of the organisation. Does not meeting unrealistic expectations really constitute a failure of the transformation programme, or is it more a failure of understanding and leadership?

Origins of the myth

There are numerous sources quoted for this 70% failure figure – here are three of the most popular.

Reengineering the Corporation: A manifesto for business revolution by Michael Hammer and James Champy[24]

This best-selling 1993 book told how a quantum leap in performance could be achieved through the radical redesign of a company's processes, organisation and culture, with Hammer and Champy concluding:

> 'Our unscientific estimate is that as many as 50 percent to 70 percent of the organizations that undertake a reengineering effort do not achieve the dramatic results they intended.'

Their 'unscientific estimate' took on an unintended life of its own, with the 70% figure starting to be quoted in multiple publications. So much so that in his subsequent 1995 book, *The Reengineering Revolution*,[25] Michael Hammer refers to this '50-70% estimate' and tries to put the record straight, saying:

> 'Unfortunately, this simple descriptive
> observation has been widely misrepresented...
> There is no inherent success or failure rate for
> reengineering.'

By then, though, the genie was well and truly out of the bottle.

Leading change: Why transformation efforts fail by John Kotter[26]

Another source is John Kotter's 'Leading change' article published in the *Harvard Business Review* in 1995, in which he talks about having watched dozens of companies undertake efforts to improve their performance via a number of different initiatives – total quality management, reengineering, right sizing, restructuring, cultural change and turnaround. He concludes:

> 'A few of these corporate change efforts have
> been very successful, a few have been utter
> failures. Most fall somewhere in between, with
> a distinct tilt toward the lower end of the scale.'

Nowhere in the paper is a 70% failure rate mentioned, and the paper itself is his opinion and not based on actual research. This article became one of the most popular ever featured in the Harvard Business Review and Kotter later expanded on these ideas in his book, *Leading Change*, published in 1996.[27]

Cracking the code of change by Nitin Nohria and Michael Beer[28]

A third popular source is a 2000 article by Nitin Nohria and Michael Beer entitled, 'Cracking the code of change', in which they discuss how difficult it is for companies to manage the process of change, and conclude by saying:

> 'Most of their initiatives have had low success rates. The brutal fact is that about 70% of all change initiatives fail.'

There's no ambiguity about their conclusion and the 70% figure is now well on its way to becoming accepted fact, despite there being no substantiated evidence for it.

Established 'fact'

By 2008, the 70% figure is well and truly established and being widely used. Bain & Company, a management consultancy, published a white paper entitled, 'Leading change management requires sticking to the PLOT: A framework for implementing change',[29] in which it is stated:

'People have been writing about change management for decades and still the statistics haven't improved. With each survey, 70% of change initiatives still fail.'

In 2009, McKinsey published a paper entitled 'The irrational side of change management' by Carolyn Dewar and Scott Keller.[30] In the paper, they refer to John Kotter's book, *Leading Change*, saying:

'Considered by many to be the seminal work in the field of change management, Kotter's research revealed that only 30 percent of change programmes succeed.'

This comment is great, apart from two things:

- It wasn't research, it was his observation.
- It's not true.

The reality

Dewar and Keller's 2009 McKinsey paper also references a 2008 survey conducted by McKinsey entitled, 'Creating organisational transformation'.[31] This was a global survey sent to 3,199 executives around the world that asked about their experience of organisational transformation and concluded:

'We found, as Kotter did, that only one transformation in three succeeds.'

This is just wrong as that's not what Kotter found or said. What the McKinsey survey actually found (from those that responded) was:

- 4.88% of transformation programmes were extremely successful.

- 30.51% were very successful.

- 48.96% were somewhat successful.

- 5.87% were not successful at all.

So, approximately 35% were extremely or very successful, with nearly 49% deemed somewhat successful. What exactly this means isn't explored, but only 6% were deemed to have not been successful at all, ie failures.

Debunking the myth (and why it continues)

You may be wondering why the mythical 70% figure continues to be peddled as it's not as if there haven't been efforts to rebuke it. In addition to Michael Hammer's failed attempt in 1996, here are just two of many that can be easily found.

The first is from December 2011 by Mark Hughes of Brighton University in the UK. His research concluded:

> 'Whilst the existence of a popular narrative of 70 per cent organizational change failure is acknowledged, there is no valid and reliable empirical evidence to support such a narrative.'[32]

The second is an article from September 2019 by Dr Jen Frahm of the Agile Change Leadership Institute. The title says it all:

> '70% of change fails: Bollocks!'[33]

So why does the myth still exist?

Consultancies, particularly the larger ones, have no real interest in dispelling it. Organisations that want to transform are much more likely to engage a consultancy that states, with its help, it can avoid being among the 70% that fail. As mentioned in Chapter Three, most organisations will need additional help with their transformation programmes, but the scale of the 'help' provided by some consultancies can often be much larger – and significantly more costly – than is actually needed. Consultancies that use scare tactics to acquire business are not acting in the client's best interest.

Summary

Don't panic too much about your transformation initiative and its risk of failure. You have a much better chance of succeeding, or at least not abjectly failing, than you may have thought. However, this doesn't mean you can rest on your laurels as programmes do still fail and, as we'll see in the next chapter, sometimes quite spectacularly.

Key points

- It's a myth that 70% of transformation programmes fail.

- There's a big difference between not meeting unrealistic expectations and failing.

- Don't be pressured into buying consultancy services on the premise that you'll fail without them.

Food for thought

- Have consultancies ever played on the '70% fail' card in an effort to win your business – and have you bought services on that basis?

- Have transformation programmes you've been involved with fully delivered the initial benefits expected?

8
It'll Never Happen To Us

In this chapter we:

- Look at a couple of case studies of major transformation failures

- Highlight the transformation icebergs ($\triangle$) – the things that should have raised red flags and prompted further investigation and action

Fancy explaining to your board and shareholders how you managed to waste over £100 million and years of time and effort? It won't be you, right? I'm sure that thought never crossed the minds of those in charge of the transformation initiatives at Co-op Insurance and Lidl – but it happened.

No one sets out to fail but the examples below show that it does happen, and it will continue to happen until transformational change is better understood. It needs to be approached and executed in the right way, with solid foundations laid and leaders providing clear vision and direction, ensuring that focus on outcomes is maintained throughout the transformation journey.

Co-op Insurance and IBM

The origin of the project

Co-op Bank nearly collapsed in 2013 until a rescue plan was devised to turn around the business. Part of the turnaround plan included overhauling its creaking IT infrastructure after years of underinvestment[34] and cancelling the planned sale of its general insurance business, CIS General Insurance Ltd (CISGIL), which traded as Co-op Insurance.[35]

This was followed by an announcement in June 2015 that CISGIL had entered into a £55 million deal with IBM for a new integrated insurance platform.[36] At the time, CISGIL CEO Mark Summerfield said:

> 'The capabilities delivered by the new IT platform will allow us to increase the number of Co-operative customers and members we serve, both through competitive propositions and through the development of strong distribution and insurer partnerships.'[37]

The ten-year deal would see IBM run the platform under a managed service contract, with IBM subcontracting the provision of the platform's software to The Innovation Group.[38] The deal was part of Co-op's Project Cobalt – the wider transformation programme to migrate its general insurance business from the legacy IT infrastructure it shared with the Co-op Bank to a new, modern insurance platform.[39]

The technology platform was to be completed in three stages. Release one would go live in March 2016, release two in August 2016 and release three no later than November 2017. The platform would be used for all insurance operations including new business processing, claims processing, policy serving, interfacing with third parties and hosting services. CISGIL would pay IBM a further £125.6 million to maintain the system for the next ten years.[40]

The downfall of the project

IBM had subcontracted £45 million of software from The Innovation Group, the intention being that CISGIL would use The Innovation Group's Insurer Suite platform. But IBM failed to meet the release one deadline due to delays caused by The Innovation Group, and in a revised plan said that it would instead be delivered in part by June 2017.[41] IBM also missed this deadline, and as they were unable to hit agreed milestones, this put them in breach of the contract (they were liable for The Innovation Group's performance).[41]

△ 1

Given the size of the programme, only having three releases should have raised concerns about the delivery approach. Where are the quick wins, the incremental and smaller-scale deliverables that could be implemented and start adding value without having to be part of one of three big releases? Also, although it's not clear how much work was done before the announcement of the deal in June 2015, for the first release (ie the one that implements all the base infrastructure and applications etc) to be completed by March 2016 should have rung alarm bells as being far too optimistic. Was this a date given by IBM and not challenged by CISGIL, or was it dictated by the CISGIL leadership team with challenges dismissed? That it was unrealistic was shown to be the case by the subsequent moving of the live date to June 2017, some fifteen months later... and that was only a partial release (which they also failed to deliver on time).

CISGIL subsequently rejected an invoice for almost £3 million from IBM on a technicality as it did not contain a purchase order number. CISGIL had in fact refused to provide IBM with a purchase order number, stating that the invoice was not due as IBM had not hit earlier contractual milestones. After CISGIL's non-payment of the invoice, IBM claimed that it was contractually entitled to cease work on the project and terminated the contract in July 2017.[42]

The legal fallout

In January 2018, CISGIL filed a £128 million lawsuit against IBM for terminating the contract and tried to claim all wasted project costs. It also filed a lesser claim of £16 million for additional costs incurred.[43] As part of the lawsuit, CISGIL claimed that:

- The Innovation Group did not have a configurable software product capable of meeting contractual requirements.[44]

- IBM had not adequately reviewed The Innovation Group to determine its suitability for the project and that its Insurer Suite would need significant changes to the base code to be suitable for CISGIL's needs.[45]

- If CISGIL had known the IT system wasn't an off-the-shelf product, they would not have taken out the contract with IBM.[46/Δ2]

- IBM failed to meet reporting requirements and were responsible for delays.[47]

- The white-label insurance platform offered by The Innovation Group was built with the US market in mind and IBM had failed to properly assess the suitability of the Insurer Suite software product for the UK insurance market.[48/Δ3]

- The costs incurred by CISGIL in relation to the contract were now wasted as a result of the non-delivery of the solution.[49]

△ 2

Why didn't CISGIL know that the system they were buying wasn't an off-the-shelf product and required significant changes to the base code to be suitable? This was intended to be CISGIL's strategic platform so I'd have thought they would have taken an interest. These are basic due diligence questions that should have been asked. Did no one in the CISGIL leadership or programme teams think it would be a good idea to check that what was being bought could do the job required? Or did they ask IBM only to be told 'Yes it can' and take that at face value without understanding what that actually meant (ref Chapter Three)?

△ 3

As for being designed for the US rather than the UK insurance market, did no one within CISGIL know that there's a difference in how those two markets work or, if they didn't know, find out, just in case? Not knowing this is an absolute failure in their due diligence process as this should have been a huge red flag.

In a counterclaim, IBM claimed that they were owed the £3 million for the unpaid invoice. Overall, it was ruled that:

- IBM was not in breach of contract in relation to the suitability of the system but was responsible for the critical delays to the project and had not satisfied its contractual reporting requirements.

- IBM's invoice had become payable pursuant to the contractual milestone payments and was not paid.

- IBM did not have the right to terminate the contract when it did because CISGIL followed the contractual mechanism to dispute the invoice, therefore CISGIL's non-payment did not constitute a repudiatory breach.

- The judge was in favour of CISGIL for its lesser claim for just under £15.9 million, reduced to £12.9 million following the offset of IBM's invoice.

- CISGIL's primary claim for its wasted costs of £128 million did not succeed because of the limitation of liability in the contract that prevented CISGIL from recovering 'loss of profit, revenue or savings', and the judge decided CISGIL's wasted costs fell into this category.[50]

In January 2020, CISGIL sued IBM for £155 million as they were dissatisfied with the result of the first lawsuit.[51] Prior to these proceedings, the Co-op Group had sold its insurance business for £185 million to Markerstudy (CISGIL is now Soteria Insurance Ltd).[52] The sale of CISGIL followed a 21% drop in sales during the first half of 2017, which contributed to an operating loss before tax of £15.5 million and a £7.6 million underwriting loss.[53]

On 4 April 2022, it was ruled that IBM must pay a further £80.6 million to CISGIL. Most of the appeal by

CISGIL was based on overturning the original judge's interpretation of the liability clause, but the appeal judge also stated that if the project had succeeded, CISGIL's profits would have increased by approximately £4 million a year, so the company may have been sold for a higher price or may not have been sold at all.[54]

Lidl and SAP

The origin of the project

The Schwarz Group, the owner of the Lidl and Kaufland brands and one of the largest retailers in the world, generated €133.6 billion worth of sales in 2021 – approximately 75% of this total was carried out under the Lidl brand.[55] But in previous years, Lidl had been making headlines for lagging in the race to digitise its back-office procedures,[56] as its legacy system for merchandise management, Wawi, was hampered by process breaks, redundant master data storage, integration gaps and functional restrictions. The system was becoming increasingly difficult to run and maintain due to multiple interfaces and modules as well as a decentralised server structure.[57]

SAP SE (SAP) is a German-based multinational software corporation that makes enterprise software to manage business operations and customer relations.

In 2011, Lidl began developing a new solution nick-named 'eLWIS' (Elektronische Lidl Warenwirtschafts Informations System, pronounced Elvis in German)[58] which was an adaptation of the SAP Retail product. Although unconfirmed by both Lidl and SAP, the implementation is thought to have cost around €500 million and involved over a thousand staff members and hundreds of external consultants.[59/Δ4] German management consultancy KPS was the primary group responsible for guiding Lidl through its business transformation from its legacy software to a new target operating model, supported by eLWIS.[60]

△ 4

By any measure, this was a huge programme – over a thousand staff and hundreds of external consultants. They *may* have all been necessary, but it feels like a lot of people. Was there really sufficient visibility and control over the programme? Did anyone know what all these people were doing, or were they just 'doing stuff'?

May 2015 saw eLWIS go live in Austrian stores following pilot phases in the United States and Northern Ireland, where Lidl had smaller operations.[61] The ultimate goal was for the system to be rolled out to 10,000 stores and more than 140 logistic hubs. The system was in place for three years and, from the outside, it looked like all was going smoothly, with SAP even awarding Lidl a prize in April 2017 for being one of their best customers.[62]

The downfall of the project

In July 2018, seven years after the work began and three years after the go-live in Austria, Lidl announced they were terminating the project and the implementation of eLWIS.[63] Lidl's CEO at the time, Jesper Hoyer, sent an internal memo to staff stating that the strategic goals, as originally defined by the project, could not be achieved without the retailer having to spend more than it wanted.[64/△5]

△ 5

How could it have possibly taken so long for Lidl to realise the programme wasn't financially viable? How often was the ongoing viability of the programme assessed and at what stage did the expected cost to completion outweigh the projected benefits? It looks as if there was very poor control over programme progress and costs, so Lidl just kept on going, or, if the information was available, it never reached the right people for informed decisions to be made.

The beginning of the end of the project was when Lidl refused to change its inventory management system to align to the capabilities of SAP Retail. In a method rather unique to Lidl and unlike many of its competitors, Lidl bases its inventory management system on purchase prices, but the standard SAP Retail software uses retail prices. Lidl believed that their use of purchase prices was one of the contributing factors to their success and maintaining their competitive advantage when it came to keeping prices low for their customers. Lidl, therefore, declined to change to the standard used by SAP and instead asked that the software be adapted to their needs.[65/Δ6] But the software was not designed to make the increasingly complex accommodations that Lidl was asking for, which led to it being more susceptible to failure and poor performance, and the project becoming more expensive than originally anticipated.[66]

△ 6

It's all very well wanting to do something differently, however, the gap (chasm!) between how Lidl operated and how SAP Retail worked should have been identified as a possible major issue at the start of the programme and fully investigated. If the extent of changes necessary was at least partially understood at the outset, would Lidl have gone down the SAP route? Where was the due diligence to assess whether SAP was fit-for-purpose, or was it just presumed that, as SAP is such a well-known company, it would all be OK? Did KPS provide any assurance? Also, at various stages during the programme, as the need for greater customisation became apparent and costs were increasing, were any questions asked about the ongoing viability of the programme? It seems not.

When they aborted the eLWIS project, Lidl decided to revert to their old system, Wawi – the one previously deemed to be no longer suitable. Wawi was now going to be the basis for Lidl's modernisation, and they decided that they were going to develop it further.[67] A company insider told the German business paper *Handelsblatt*, 'We are practically starting from scratch.'[68] Lidl claimed that it was not a decision against SAP, but for its own system, and that they would continue to work closely with SAP in other areas.[69]

Contributing factors to the failure

A primary cause of the failure was Lidl's 'but this is how we always do it' stance and the expectation to be able to adapt SAP Retail to a system based on purchase prices rather than retail prices. A requirement gap of that size and the lack of compatibility between Lidl's needs and SAP Retail's capabilities should have been identified and assessed in the project's very early stages. The amount of customisation needed saw Lidl with a product with declining performance and a project with massively rising costs. IT experts described the changes needed to SAP Retail like changing a prefab house – you can put the kitchen cupboards in a different place, but when you start moving the walls, there's no stability.

But SAP only provided the software – it was KPS's responsibility to manage the implementation and the process of adapting the software to Lidl's needs. KPS was later accused of being too slow,[70] but KPS claims that even though they were working on shorter deadlines than other projects of a similar nature, their pilots still ran on time and the blame for delays lay elsewhere.[71]

It's hard to imagine that turnover in Lidl's executive team helped the project in any way, as maintaining momentum and keeping newcomers invested with personal buy-in is difficult to do with constant change. In March 2014, Lidl's CEO Karl-Heinz Holland departed the company abruptly after six years as CEO, citing 'unbridgeable differences over future strategy'.[72] In February 2017, Sven Seidel resigned as Lidl's CEO after only three years and was replaced by Jesper Hoyer, who cancelled a number of other planned digital initiatives as well as eLWIS.[73] By May 2017, Lidl's Head of IT, Alexander Sonnenmoser, had also left.[74]

The project began in 2011 and was abandoned in 2018 – a window of seven years in which the company's needs were not being fully met. It's an expensive lesson but, given Lidl's resources, not one that threatened its existence. Since 2018, Lidl has continued to invest in its infrastructure and services, and in 2022 became the first UK supermarket to trial on-shelf smart refills.[75]

Summary

These are just two examples of large-scale, high-profile transformation failures. They highlight a number of reasons why initiatives can fail, from poor executive leadership to some pretty basic howlers – not sufficiently understanding whether the shiny new technology you've just bought is fit-for-purpose, poor due diligence, etc. And if litigation ever becomes a serious option, it's likely to be indicative of a major failing of governance and leadership.

Smaller-scale failures also occur but these don't tend to make such a splash in the public domain. More often than not they are quietly brushed under the carpet and, understandably, not openly discussed. Lidl may be able to afford to write off €500 million but for many smaller organisations, a few hundred thousand pounds may be enough to sink them. This is why, although getting transformational change right may seem expensive, it's a false economy to think it can be done successfully 'on the cheap' – it can't.

These examples are undoubtedly complex, costly and occurred over many years. However, there are some basic principles of good and best practice that, if followed, may have negated, or at least minimised, the impact of these failures – we'll discuss these in the next chapter.

Key points

- Don't be complacent about any type of transformation – it's complex and it can go horribly wrong.

- Make sure you understand what you're getting into and that contractual arrangements are clear for all parties – litigation is never a good place to end up.

- You wouldn't build or buy a house without solid foundations, so why potentially spend millions on a transformation programme without them?

- Don't try to be too clever or succumb to Magpie Syndrome, ie don't chase after the shiny stuff and neglect practical activities that can genuinely improve services and add value.[76]

- Beware false economies.

Food for thought

- Have you ever been part of a transformation programme that's gone off the rails and, with hindsight, what could have been done to prevent it from happening?

- Have you ever been too gung-ho and proceeded with an initiative without doing appropriate due diligence?

- Does your organisation have an effective governance structure in place to minimise the risk of making unwise decisions?

9
The Basics

In this chapter we:

- Look at aspects of good and best practice that should be applied to any project or programme

- Highlight areas that are particularly relevant to transformational change

The transformation programme failures in the previous chapter weren't inevitable, but they ended up being spectacularly costly. There are, of course, ways to guarantee failure. For example, ill-thought-through targets and poorly designed reward mechanisms can drive bad behaviours – a CEO's bonus may be dependent on getting something live by a certain date, regardless of whether it's ready or properly tested. The following months or even years may be spent remediating a wholly self-inflicted and avoidable problem, possibly at huge financial and reputational cost (to the organisation, not necessarily the CEO).

However, organisations can give themselves a much better chance of transformation success by simply getting the basics right, or in some cases making sure they're actually done in the first place. The basics outlined below aren't a 'how to' guide for managing projects and programmes – there is lots of material available that addresses that – but they describe aspects of good and best practice that should be applied to projects and programmes of any size, regardless of methodology. And if applied *sensibly* and *appropriately* they will significantly increase your chances of success – ignore them at your peril.

Describe the desired outcomes (and why you want them)

Ensure you have a clear vision and can articulate the outcomes you want for your organisation. At a high level, define the overall programme objectives and key results (OKRs) and what success looks like. You don't need detail, just a clear understanding of *what* you want to achieve, ie the *outcomes*, not possible solutions.

Make sure you understand *why* the initiative is required. Is it really what the organisation needs at this time? Does it really address the problems that need to be solved? The reasons for undertaking the initiative, whatever they may be, must have a sound basis – vanity projects may be great for a CEO's ego, but they are unlikely to be good for the organisation.

Be realistic

It's important to set realistic objectives and expectations. Transformation initiatives will have many unknowns and assumptions at the outset – you need to accept there will be a high degree of uncertainty.

Resist the temptation to set arbitrary delivery dates, ignore bandwagons and don't succumb to the fear of missing out (FOMO). Just because it seems that everyone else is doing something is not a good reason to do it too. It may, of course, be just what's needed but, if you want to avoid failure, go through the process of ensuring it's the right thing to do for the organisation first.

Transformation programmes are complex. Be aware of what you're getting into and accept that there will be some hard decisions and compromises to make along the way. The scale of change involved and its impact on all areas of the organisation is not to be underestimated.

Define the scope

Regardless of the programme methodology (waterfall, agile, a hybrid model, etc) the scope needs to be defined to a sufficient degree. If the programme scope isn't known, you won't understand what needs to be done, nor be able to identify the impact of change on the organisation or who needs to be involved.

When defining the scope, don't lose sight of the big picture and the overall outcomes, and remember that it may initially involve numerous assumptions, which should be reviewed regularly. One of the major contributors to programmes going off track is scope creep, where requirements are continually added to or changed. Controlling the scope with clear direction, effective governance, a fit-for-purpose change control process and firm but fair programme leadership and stakeholder management is crucial.

Develop a business and benefits case

The primary point of a business case is to make a compelling argument for something to be done. At a high level it should describe what the thing is, why it should be done and what alternative options were considered, as well as the viability of doing it.

There should be a positive benefits case, where total benefits outweigh total costs over the chosen period.[77] As well as the programme costs, you need to consider the ongoing post-live operational and support costs. Include tangible and intangible costs and benefits – including the costs and benefits of doing nothing.

To illustrate the intangible aspect, ie where it's difficult to attribute a specific financial value, think about a mandatory change that has to be made, for example, because of new regulation. You may wonder how a positive cost-benefit case can be established, as it's going to cost you to implement the change, and for what benefit? Well, in this case, the benefit would be the ability to continue trading or to avoid a financial penalty and the accompanying reputational damage.

There are numerous ways to calculate the potential return and viability of a programme, including:

- Return on investment (ROI)[78]
- Internal rate of return (IRR)[79]
- Payback period (PP)[80]
- Discounted payback period (DPP)[81]

Business stakeholders that may be impacted by the change and the finance team should also be involved in developing business cases – it is not just a project or programme activity.

Given the scale of change that may be involved, along with the lack of firm information and initial uncertainty, establishing costs and benefits for a transformation initiative can be challenging. Be assured, though, that whatever you come up with initially is probably going to be wrong. You are likely to be over-optimistic – you'll probably underestimate the costs and start accounting for benefits too early. On the positive side though, you may also underestimate the overall benefits that will be realised over time (assuming the programme is successful, of course).

Get buy-in

Transformation initiatives need buy-in at the executive level, but bear in mind that the leadership team is likely to have differing areas of interest and focus. The CFO (chief financial officer) will have a different perspective and different priorities from the CIO (chief information officer) and COO (chief operating officer), etc.

Despite the different possible perspectives, the executive team must be united about the transformation initiative – its overall objectives and goals, and the broad approach to it. A divided board will be unable to provide the clear direction needed and, without this, it will be near impossible to get lower levels of the organisation onside. This can result in confusion, uncertainty, in-fighting and politicking, leading to slow programme progress, decisions not being made, etc, with anticipated benefits unlikely to be achieved.

Recognise too that people have different ways of learning, absorbing and processing information. Getting buy-in at all levels of the organisation may require a variety of engagement and awareness-raising activities and techniques – a weekly email to all staff is not sufficient.

Identify stakeholders

People and teams at all levels across the organisation can be impacted in different ways. There will be different perspectives, none of which should be instantly dismissed. Spend time early on identifying the different stakeholder groups and determine, with their input, what their interests and concerns are and how best to involve and communicate with them. This will help to avoid alienating people and provide an early indication of the mood of the organisation regarding the proposed initiative, particularly what sort of reluctance and resistance there may be.

Understand customer needs

Identify the different customer groups that may be impacted and establish, where appropriate, how best to engage, involve or communicate with them. To understand what customers need you should, of course, ask them what they want, but only as a way to discover *what they want to achieve* and the *problems they have trying to achieve it*. Resulting solutions should address these aspects, which may not necessarily be what customers say they want.

A quote that's often wrongly attributed to Henry Ford (founder of the Ford Motor Company) illustrates this:

'If I had asked customers what they wanted, they would have said faster horses.'

171

What Ford did say though was:

> 'If there was any one secret of success, it lies in the ability to get the other person's point of view and see things from that person's angle as well as from your own.'[82]

Now that's how to understand your customers.

Customer journeys may change, but mapping them should not be done in isolation. Ensure any journey mapping activity is incorporated as part of the wider end-to-end process work – it all needs to join up.

Communicate

If you know who is impacted and how, communicate with them. Keep them appropriately informed. Remember, transformation is a journey – colleagues, customers, suppliers and third parties may all be impacted, and you need to take them with you. Core messages should be consistent, but be aware that because of their differing interests, the level of detail and content of messages should be tailored to each stakeholder group.

Create a communication plan employing different ways of disseminating information and establish feedback mechanisms and encourage their use – communication is two-way after all. Communication from the leadership and programme teams should involve regular, simple and consistent messages. Effective communication is vital to mitigate reluctance and resistance to change. It won't solve all issues, but it will go a long way to help.

The point of communicating is to inform people about something or to ask them to do something. If the programme would like something to be done, particularly if it's important, it is not sufficient to send an email and then expect it to be done – it's still OK to talk to people!

Manage third parties (and avoid being exploited)

If you're undertaking a transformation initiative, you will inevitably need to work with external parties, and it's vital to clearly articulate what you want from them. When you have engaged their services you should also minimise their wriggle room – define their involvement as clearly as you can so that they stick to their brief. This will prevent you potentially being exploited.

Ensure anything being provided by an external party is detailed in an appropriate contract or statement of work. Wherever possible, use your own contracts, not those from the third party. There may be multiple contracts with multiple suppliers for specialist products and services – seek expert legal advice when negotiating these. This is important for both parties as, if things don't work out as expected, there will be pre-agreed escape routes – litigation is never a desired outcome.

There may also be multiple contracts with a single supplier covering, for example:

- The licensing of software

- Implementation activity (programme services, configuration, integration, migration, etc)

- Use and support of systems post-implementation

Every contract should have provisions for performance and, if underperforming, defined means of resolution and ultimately viable means of exit for all parties. Make sure you read and fully understand any contracts before signing them and always be prepared to walk away regardless of how far through the negotiation process you are. As unpalatable as that may seem, it will be far less painful than signing up to something that you cannot get out of or is too one-sided and has you over a barrel.

Don't take everything you're told by consultancies and solution providers at face value. Ask questions, seek proof, and ask more questions to determine what's true and what's not. Does that functionality really exist? Do they actually have that capability or is it just smoke and mirrors?

Before engaging external parties, consider what you can do internally. Do you really need that team of expensive consultants now or are there things that you can do before getting them in? The answer is there's a lot you can probably do that will not only save you money but will also put you in a much better position once you do engage third parties, eg making sure you understand your business model and defining your current operating model.

One of the risks of engaging solution providers and consultancies too soon is that they may take advantage of any lack of preparedness, and you'll end up with a much larger team than necessary. This will be great for their revenue stream but not so good for your business case.

Define roles and responsibilities

Once you have established clear direction and programme objectives, define, agree and communicate roles and responsibilities to all parties involved so everyone knows who's doing what and what's expected of them. Using the RACI model is an effective way of doing this. It simply states, for a given activity:

- **R** – Who is **responsible** for its completion (there may be more than one person or team responsible)

- **A** – Who is **accountable** for its completion (there should be a single person accountable)

- **C** – Who should be **consulted** to get their input

- **I** – Who should be **informed** of the activity being done

With multiple parties involved in any transformation programme, it's imperative to understand who is doing what so work isn't duplicated, or not done at all.

Agree programme methodology and approach

When establishing the programme, ensure it is structured appropriately to reflect what needs to be done. Don't impose artificial boundaries on the programme structure or insist on a particular methodology – despite the many advantages of an agile approach, not everything is best done in an agile way. There are a multitude of ways to do things, so use whichever tools and techniques are best for the job. Approaches should be outlined and agreed for:

- Programme management and delivery

- Communication

- Software development and integration

- Testing

- Data migration

- People

- Deployment, transition to and embedding within the BAU operation

The overall duration of transformation initiatives can be lengthy, so it's important to build a realistic expectation of pace into programmes to ensure that any 'quick wins' can be realised as soon as sensibly possible.

The scale of the programme may warrant a dedicated transformation programme management office (TPMO) function being set up. This should be established with a clearly defined remit and responsibilities that are aligned to the transformation programme objectives.

Establish appropriate programme governance

Effective programme governance is essential to ensure all parties are clear about how the programme operates – this does not mean lots of red tape. Effective governance, administered through a PMO or TPMO function, provides structure, control and visibility over all programme activities, including:

- Programme progress and reporting

- Management of programme risks, issues, assumptions and dependencies

- Cost and benefits management

- Procedures for change control, approvals, escalation, etc

Having accurate information is vital to ensure that reporting on every aspect of the programme is up to date and correct. This means that everyone knows what's going on as well as being able to determine the ongoing viability of the programme. Information should be clear, concise and relevant – there is no prize for the biggest reporting pack.

Corporate culture is an important factor in the successful running of any transformation programme. Given the nature of transformational change, there will be times when things do not run smoothly, so when the first signs of problems arise, they need to be surfaced as early as possible so they can be resolved. If the corporate culture is such that bad news or potential bad news is dismissed or met with anger or blame, problems may be left to fester – and problems rarely age well.

When issues are identified, representatives and leaders from the business should not sit back and assume that it's the programme's responsibility to sort out. Any transformation initiative should be for the benefit of the organisation as a whole and everyone needs to work together, collaboratively, to resolve difficulties – they can't just be viewed as the programme's responsibility.

Agree plans

Have a delivery plan (the stuff to do) and a benefits realisation plan (when you expect to start reaping benefits). For the delivery plan, regardless of methodology, you need to know what's being done, who's doing it and when it will be completed. At the programme level don't make it too detailed, otherwise it will be unmanageable. Keep the big picture in mind so you don't lose sight of the overall objectives.

The benefits realisation plan should be aligned to the delivery plan. It is one of the ways to track the success (or otherwise) of the programme, particularly in identifying whether any quick wins actually materialise. Incurred costs, burn rates, the cost to completion and realised benefits should be periodically reviewed with reference back to the business case to assess the ongoing viability of the programme.

When creating plans, consult all the people that need to be involved. Do not guess at effort, timescale or costs or benefits on behalf of others. There will be many potential contributors to the plans – include them all. Make plans as realistic as possible, while being aware that at the outset there is likely to be a lot of uncertainty. This if fine as it will firm up as the programme progresses.

Identify assumptions and dependencies (including on external parties) and regularly review them.

Assumptions and dependencies are often poorly managed but can have a significant material impact on the programme.

At the outset, also review the organisation's existing change agenda to determine what other projects and programmes are going on. Does it make sense for them all to continue? Can some of them be consumed into the transformation programme or be deferred or stopped?

Establish appropriate and effective leadership

Transformation programmes need to be led and not just managed. Leadership particularly needs to be present at the senior levels (outlined below), and should be clear, focused and firm, although flexible enough to adapt to new information and changing circumstances.

Executive board

Given the nature of transformational change and its impact on the entire organisation, it's imperative that the programme is fully understood and supported by the executive board, as it is the board that will need to collectively make sound decisions and set a clear direction. For this to be achievable, it should be suitably diverse and all functions across the organisation should be represented. Ideally, there should also be a balanced mix of the ways in which board members are most inclined to make an impact (more on this below in 'Let's talk about…').

Programme sponsor

Appointed by the executive board, the programme sponsor is the senior person accountable for the successful delivery of the programme. Although they should work closely with the programme director, their remit is not a 'hands-on', day-to-day programme role, but they play a crucial part in the success, or otherwise, of the programme. Unfortunately, the sponsor role is often performed by a senior person with minimal understanding of what it entails and little to no experience of transformational change – this is discussed further in the next chapter.

Programme board

The programme board contains senior representatives from all key programme areas, including the main vendors and solution providers.

Programme director

Acting with the authority of the executive board, the programme director has overall responsibility for the day-to-day running of the programme, driving it forward in the direction set by the board.

LET'S TALK ABOUT... THE GC INDEX®[83]

To understand and create well-balanced and effective teams, be they executive leadership teams or programme teams, a useful tool is the GC Index®.

The GC Index® isn't a personality or psychometric test but a people and organisation profiling tool. It describes five ways (proclivities) that individuals are inclined and energised to make an impact, ie where they can be most effective and productive. It's used by small and large organisations across the world, including Deloitte, Santander, AstraZeneca, Puma, NHS, FTI and Danske Bank, amongst many others.

The five ways that individuals can make an impact, Figure 31, are:

- *Game Changers* generate the ideas and possibilities that have the potential to be transformational.

- *Strategists* see the future, bring clear direction and apply ideas within a strategic context.

- *Implementers* get things done, shape strategic plans and deliver tangible outcomes.

- *Polishers* create a future to be proud of and make things better with continual improvement.

- *Play Makers* bring people and teams together, orchestrating activities to achieve desired objectives.

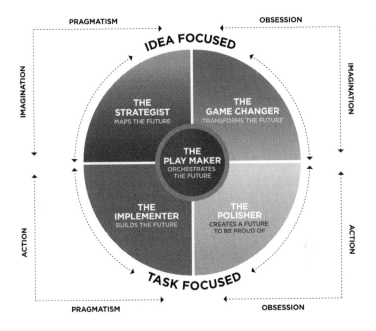

Figure 31: The five GC Index® ways to make an impact.

The GC Index® scores each proclivity out of ten, with the two highest defining an individual's strongest areas of impact – I am a Play Maker-Strategist. It is not a measure of someone's ability to do a job, and a low score doesn't mean they can't do something or are bad at doing it. They may be brilliant at it, but it's just not something they would choose to do – they have little inclination, energy or enthusiasm for doing it.

The GC Index® can be used in a variety of ways across an organisation, but from a transformation perspective, the focus is on the make-up of the leadership and programme teams, and trying to answer the following questions:

- Is there sufficient balance within the leadership team so the best decisions can be made?
- Are the right people in the right programme roles?

When individuals' GC Index® scores are aggregated, team views can be produced, Figure 32. This provides an objective basis for discussion about a team's potential impact. A team lacking in a particular proclivity may struggle to be truly effective, and knowing this can help establish more impactful teams. For example, if you had a leadership team with a low Game Changer score, you may question whether new and creative ideas would be given appropriate consideration. Would there really be sufficient interest in and recognition of the importance of innovative ideas and creative thinking if the leadership team, ie the decision makers, had little interest, energy or inclination for this themselves?

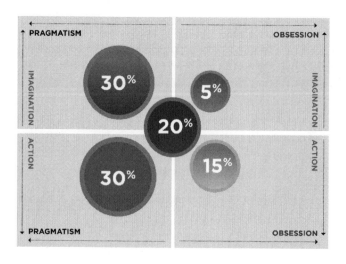

Figure 32: A GC Index® team view.

Evaluate capability

Transformational change can't be approached and treated like non-transformational change. It's more complex and requires specific expertise to orchestrate the wide range of activities and interactions involved. Realistically appraise your internal programme and change capability and determine where gaps exist from management, execution and delivery perspectives. Bear in mind that capability may not just be needed for the duration of the programme but also to support, maintain and effect change in the BAU environment after it has ended.

Summary

So, will adhering to these basics guarantee your initiative is going to be successful? Well, no, but ignoring them will certainly create problems and significantly increase the risk of failing.

There are no secrets surrounding these basics. They are well-known, established principles, and getting them right is fundamental to the success of any project or programme – they're just good practice.

But with transformation initiatives, adhering to good and best practice isn't always enough. The continued number of programmes that fail to deliver to their full potential is testament to that. So why does this continue to happen? In the next chapter, we'll look at why this is the case.

Key points

- Ignore the basics at your peril.

- Don't jump on bandwagons, there are no silver bullets.

- Always seek to establish clarity but embrace ambiguity when it arises – which will be often!

Food for thought

- Are these basic principles of good and best practice defined within your organisation's change framework?

- Are you aware of initiatives that failed because the basics weren't followed?

10
A Transformation Lens

In this chapter we:

- Look at the common reasons given for transformation programmes failing

- Explore why transformational change is often underestimated

- See why a transformation lens is required and how it can be applied

Scan the QR code to watch the accompanying video.

By now you should have a better appreciation of transformational change and a greater understanding of what it involves, ie significant changes to an organisation's business and operating models. This encompasses what it does and how it does it – the shape and structure of the organisation, its people, customers, operation and technology, and the interaction between these components.

When you add in the management of internal and external stakeholders, solution providers and other third parties, and balance these elements with changes to the organisational mindset and culture, in addition to complying with regulatory requirements, you can see that it's complex with many interconnected parts.

Despite the complexity, transformation programmes should be more successful than they often turn out to be, so what's going on?

Symptoms or causes?

We saw in Chapter One that the reasons often given for transformation initiatives failing, or not being fully successful, are symptoms rather than root causes and include:

- Unclear goals, lack of a shared direction

- Lack of buy-in from senior management

- Lack of expertise

- Unclear starting point, starting with technology

- Not understanding customer needs, ignoring customer experience

- Setting too fast a pace and not bringing people with you, not engaging with people

- Not changing the culture, internal resistance

- Assuming transformation is a one-off activity

- Not being able to measure success

Whereas there are only two root causes that need to be addressed to give your programme the greatest chance of success:

- Root Cause 1 – A lack of understanding of what transformational change involves and its impact on the organisation

- Root Cause 2 – Inappropriate capability to deliver transformational change

But what gives rise to these root causes? Why is the transformation journey often perceived to be a smooth, meandering road, Figure 33 (top), when it's more accurately represented by the bottom image – an uneven path, hard to navigate and treacherous in places?

Figure 33: An idealistic representation of the transformation journey (top)[84] and a more realistic one (bottom).[85]

The right perspective

A lot of change happens inside organisations. It may take the form of tactical change, such as process and continuous improvement, as well as more strategic change agreed as part of an organisation's periodic planning cycle. But a lot of this strategic change activity focuses on specific areas and uses existing BAU and change capability – it's not transformational. For example:

- Implementing a new HR system may enable the HR department to work more efficiently, but the impact outside of the department will be limited.

- Adhering to new regulatory legislation may involve changing some processes or introducing new ones, but it wouldn't necessarily change the purpose of the processes.

- Introducing a new version of a product may involve developing, testing, marketing and launching it, but this would just use the organisation's existing capabilities.

None of these would necessarily have a significant impact on the organisation's business model or operating model, and could probably be executed quite happily as non-transformational projects or programmes.

Now, organisations don't tend to genuinely transform very often, so when transformational change is needed, it can be incorrectly viewed and treated as 'just change', ie non-transformational rather than transformational change.

Why is this?

When you look at any situation, you do so through your own personal lens – your individually tinted spectacles. The tint on your lenses is a mix of your experience, training, and how you're wired and a host of other factors. The key thing to appreciate is that what you perceive and understand about how things are and how they work will not be entirely the same as anyone else's. Of course, there will be lots of commonality, but there will inevitably be things that we see differently because our lenses are different, such as the level of risk involved in doing something, the right approach to take, the opportunities and challenges of doing so, and so on.

Peoples' careers are often forged in function verticals, eg finance, IT, HR, etc, and our lenses are tinted accordingly. So if you're asked about something outside of your experience, you will inevitably look at it through your individual lens – it's not a question of good or bad or right or wrong, it's just how it is.

With transformation initiatives, the ideas, strategy, approach, direction and key decisions will be set by the leadership team, which is likely to be comprised of a CFO (who has come via a finance function), a CIO (technology), a COO (operations), and a CEO who may well have performed one of these roles previously. There is often little horizontal perspective that cuts across the verticals, ie no holistic, cross-functional view – no transformation lens, Figure 34. There is likely to be a lack of understanding of what's involved with transformational change and its impact on the organisation will be underestimated, as will the challenges and complexities that may be faced.

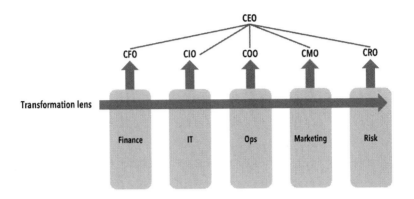

Figure 34: A transformation lens helps understand the impact of transformational change across the organisation.

Let's look at this from a different angle. If I was describing mountain climbing, Figure 35, I may use the left-hand image to convey the gist of what mountain climbing is all about, ie getting to the summit. But you wouldn't think that the straight arrow was the route a climber would actually take. You'd know the route would be more like the one in the right-hand image – sometimes going sideways, sometimes down. It would be much more complicated but necessary to achieve the objective of getting to the top.

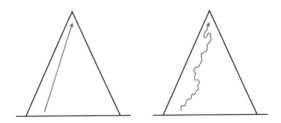

Figure 35: A representation of an ascent route (left) vs the actual route (right).

Even though most people have never been mountain climbing, it's easy to understand that there is a difference between conveying the gist and the reality of the ascent route. With transformational change though, given the complexities and the fact that it's not a common occurrence, there is often no easily available mental picture of what's involved or how to do it, so the gist – the straight arrow or the smooth road – is wrongly used to represent reality.

This can lead to oversimplifying and underestimating what's involved and is an example of *substitution bias* (also known as attribute substitution), where something complex and difficult to grasp is substituted with something easier to understand, ie transformational change is substituted with non-transformational change.

To mitigate this, you need a transformation lens so that those accountable and responsible for the success of the programme can have as great an understanding and as much information as possible at their disposal. This will enable informed decisions to be made rather than educated guesses – there's too much at stake for that.

Applying a transformation lens

A transformation lens can be applied by having real-world transformation expertise in one or more senior leadership or advisory roles, ie:

- Chief transformation or change officer (CTrO/CCO)

- Programme advisor

- Programme director

But before considering these in more detail, the role of programme sponsor needs to be discussed further.

Programme sponsor

A key role in any transformation programme is that of the sponsor – the person accountable for the programme's successful delivery, and the link between the organisation's executive board and the programme director, who has day-to-day responsibility for delivering the programme. The sponsor is the programme's highest-level leader and should have substantial interest in the programme's objectives and its success. Although it's not a hands-on role, they will be expected to:

- Be clear on what the programme is looking to achieve and why

- Obtain commitment and buy-in from senior leadership

- Obtain and commit appropriate resources (budget and people)

- Ensure the programme delivers the agreed objectives and business benefits

- Make decisions regarding programme priorities and material changes in scope and direction

- Resolve issues and conflicts and remove obstacles that are beyond the control of the programme director

- Ensure the programme is governed effectively and approve key programme deliverables

The sponsor role is vital to the smooth running of any transformation programme as well as its ultimate fate – it's not a role that should be assigned to just anyone, although it often is. The sponsor needs to have time to dedicate to the role and must understand how to perform it, its remit and boundaries. But sponsors often don't have enough transformation experience, so they'll need to draw on the experience of others to perform it effectively.

Chief transformation officer (or chief change officer)

Organisations' boards can be comprised of a wide variety of C-suite roles. Along with the traditional chief operating, information and financial officer roles (COO, CIO and CFO respectively), newer roles such as the CISO (information security), CDO (data), CCO (customer), and CSO (sustainability) are being seen more often. One of these newer roles is that of the chief transformation officer, CTrO (or chief change officer). Although not yet that common, this role's importance is being increasingly recognised due to the amount, complexity and rate of change organisations now experience.

A CTrO should have a comprehensive understanding of the challenges and complexities associated with transformational change and bring the necessary experience, horizontal view and holistic perspective to the boardroom. This will enhance the board's understanding of what's involved with transformational change and enable better informed decisions to be made about strategy, investment, approach and direction.

A 2022 study on the chief transformation officer role by Deloitte found that although there was no clear path to becoming a CTrO, the enterprise-wide nature of transformations requires cross-functional orchestration and collaboration:

> '… successful CTrOs have a range of experiences—the ability to adapt and be change-oriented and navigate multiple functions effectively… These leaders are self-aware enough to know their limitations, convene the right people, and delegate effectively.'[86]

Deloitte also notes that CTrOs require the ability for both big picture thinking and grasping the detail and structure of the business operation.

There may not be a need for a permanent or full-time CTrO – a fractional CTrO could be a viable alternative option – but they should ideally be engaged *before* any significant decisions about the transformation initiative are made.

Transformation programme advisor

If there isn't a CTrO on the organisation's board, having an independent advisor with transformation experience join the leadership team or the programme board is a pragmatic alternative. They would act as a *critical friend,* providing transformation expertise, oversight, challenge and guidance to the programme and executive boards, or they may work more closely with the programme sponsor and director if their transformation experience was limited.

Transformation programme director

The programme director has overall responsibility for the setup, execution and delivery of the programme. With transformational change, a comprehensive understanding of what's involved is a must. As the highest-ranking day-to-day member of the programme, the programme director will be the one translating the board's wishes into action and defining how the programme is structured and how it functions, as well as giving direction to the programme managers and other members of the team. It is critical to a transformation programme's success that this role is filled by a suitably experienced person.

Summary

Transformation is a complex business and is often poorly understood, so what's involved and its impact on the organisation can easily be underestimated. This, along with an often siloed and non-holistic approach, creates a recipe for disaster, with transformational change being treated as if it was non-transformational change. A transformation lens is needed for the right approach to be determined.

We'll wrap things up in the next section and recap the key factors for success.

Key points

- The typical reasons given for transformation programmes failing are symptoms, not the root causes.

- Understanding transformation requires a cross-functional, holistic view.

- What's involved with transformational change is complex and hard to visualise, so it can be wrongly perceived and treated like non-transformational change – this is an example of substitution bias.

- Key programme roles should be performed by people with transformation experience.

Food for thought

- How much transformational change experience exists within your current leadership team – does anyone provide a transformation lens?

- Have you ever been asked to sponsor a transformation programme, and if so, did you feel suitably equipped to do so?

And Finally

This brings us full circle, back to where we started, with the two root causes that need to be addressed for your transformation programme to have as great a chance of success as possible:

- Root Cause 1 – A lack of understanding of what transformational change involves and its impact on the organisation

- Root Cause 2 – Inappropriate capability to deliver transformational change

And what you need to do to address these root causes:

- Align your understanding of transformational change with your appetite for it and your expectations of it

- Align your understanding of transformational change with your capability to deliver it:
  - The experience and expertise of your resources
  - The motives of external parties (and possibly internal ones too) and how closely they align with yours

Transformation is an often misunderstood and over-used term, and transformational change is complex. There's a lot to it, and if you hadn't fully appreciated how much when you started reading this book, you will now have a far better understanding of what it is, what it involves, and the holistic approach required for it to be successful.

There are no secrets to getting this stuff right. There's no magic involved – there are no metaphorical rabbits to be pulled from the organisational hat. Transformational change simply needs to be sufficiently understood, approached and executed in the right way.

Synergies

As we saw in Chapter One, to maximise the chances of successfully transforming your organisation, you need to be at the intersection where your understanding of transformational change is aligned to your appetite for it and the capability to deliver it.

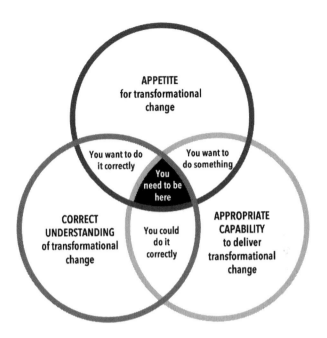

But it's not just these aspects that need to be aligned. Your organisation's vision, strategy, and target business and operating models need to be aligned, and bridged to your current business and operating models by a fit-for-purpose change roadmap and change capability. Together, these offer you the opportunity of transformation success. Remember though that no part of your organisation operates in a silo – it's all connected, and when aligned, there are synergies to be found:

- Understanding your COM enables you to confidently identify the areas impacted by change – this helps provide *operational resilience.*

- Understanding your COM, coupled with an effective change capability, enables you to react swiftly and confidently to change – this gives you *business agility*.

Whether you're thinking about embarking on a transformation initiative or not, you can achieve a lot simply by having an effective change capability, and genuinely understanding what you do now and how you do it – your current business and operating models. As I've shown, this doesn't mean you need an expensive army of consultants, just the right understanding and approach.

Points to keep in mind

If you are considering a transformation programme, keep these points in mind:

- Don't skip the basics – they're not sexy but they are essential to construct a solid foundation for change.

- Keep expectations realistic – don't jump on bandwagons.

- 'Transformational' and 'non-transformational' change are very different things.

- Recognise where internal transformation and change capability is lacking – cooking dinner for friends is not the same as hosting a banquet.

- Don't confuse being complex with being hard – anything is hard if you don't have the right experience, skills, mindset and tools.

- Seek clarity and certainty and minimise ambiguity wherever possible – but accept there will be ambiguity, particularly at the outset, and embrace it when it arises.

- If you need more information, consider whether it's detail or context that will aid understanding.

- Maintain a holistic view and never lose sight of the big picture.

- KISS! Keep things as simple as possible – they'll get complicated enough quite easily without any additional effort.

- Ask the right questions to understand the problems – if the answer is 'We need a new system', you're barking up the wrong tree.

- The lowest-cost option is not always the best – beware of false economies.

- Break down silos – organisational, operational, management and mindset.

- Transformation is a journey and you have to take people with you.

That's a wrap

I hope you've found this book informative, insightful and useful, and I'd love to hear where it's made a difference to your transformation journey, so please get in touch – my contact details are in the 'The Author' section.

Good luck with all your current and future transformation initiatives. It is possible to be successful as long as you understand what you're getting into and approach it in the right way.

Don't forget, transformational change is complex, but it doesn't have to be (that) hard!

References

All photographs and images used with permission.

1 Friends enjoying a dinner party at home, copyright 2016 Monkey Business Images/Shutterstock

2 Nobel banquet in the City Hall of Sweden, TT News Agency/Alamy Stock Photo

3 W Glaeser, 'Where does the term VUCA come from?', Vuca-World (no date), www.vuca-world.org, accessed 15 February 2023

4 WG Bennis and B Nanus, *Leaders: Strategies for taking charge* (Harper Business, 2004, first published 1985)

5 J Clear, 'This coach improved every tiny thing by 1 percent and here's what happened', JamesClear.com (no date), https://jamesclear.com/marginal-gains, accessed 15 February 2023

6 Formula 1, 'Red Bull smash pit stop world record' (2019), www.youtube.com/watch?v=BI75uWxEajA, accessed 15 February 2023

7 Formula One Pit Stop, copyright 2017 Abdul Razak Latif/Shutterstock

8 P McClean, 'Wales hospital uses F1 pit stop tactics for newborn resuscitation', *Financial Times* (2016),

www.ft.com/content/35f34152-1695-11e6-9d98-00386a18e39d, accessed 15 February 2023

9 Brooks's law isn't actually a law, it's an observation made by Frederick P. Brooks Jr in his 1975 book, *The Mythical Man-Month: Essays on software engineering* (Addison-Wesley), where he argues that adding more resources to software projects doesn't always speed things up, as the benefits of extra resources can be outweighed by increased communication issues and the additional management overhead required.

10 Inter IKEA Systems BV, 'The IKEA vision and values', ikea.com (no date), www.ikea.com/gb/en/this-is-ikea/about-us/the-ikea-vision-and-values-pub9aa779d0, accessed 15 February 2023

11 K Ohmae, cited in William J Brown, *AntiPatterns in Project Management* (Wiley, 2000), p3

12 Oxford University Press, Oxford Languages and Google, languages.oup.com (no date), https://languages.oup.com/google-dictionary-en, accessed 15 February 2023

13 Camel Taxi, copyright Banol2007/Dreamstime.com

14 Mona Lisa jigsaw, jvphoto/Alamy Stock Photo

15 S Peak, 'Keep It Simple: Why businesses need to "KISS" more and how to do it', business.com (2023), www.business.com/articles/keep-it-simple-why-businesses-need-to-kiss-more-and-how-to-do-it, accessed 15 February 2023

16 Ceramic mugs, copyright 2018 EllenM/Shutterstock

17 Simple jigsaw, copyright Bigandt/Dreamstime.com

18 Larger piece jigsaw, copyright Balky79/Dreamstime.com

19 H Robinson, 'Why do most transformations fail?', McKinsey & Company (2019), www.mckinsey.com/capabilities/transformation/our-insights/why-do-most-transformations-fail-a-conversation-with-harry-robinson, accessed 5 February 2023

20 P Forth, T Reichert, R de Laubier, S Chakraborty, 'Flipping the odds of digital transformation success', bgc.com (2019), www.bcg.com/publications/2020/increasing-odds-of-success-in-digital-transformation, accessed 15 February 2023

21 D O'Brien, 'Five ways to accelerate digital transformation', pwc.com (2020), www.pwc.com/jg/en/services/advisory/blogs/five-ways-to-accelerate-digital-transformation.html, accessed 15 February 2023

22 Deloitte MCS Limited, 'Digital transformation: Are people still our greatest asset?', Deloitte (2020), www2.deloitte.

com/content/dam/Deloitte/uk/Documents/about-deloitte/deloitte-uk-digital-transformation-are-people-still-our-greatest-asset.pdf, accessed 15 February 2023

23 Unicorn, copyright James Lee/Unsplash.com

24 M Hammer and J Champy, *Reengineering the Corporation: A manifesto for business revolution* (Harper Collins, 1993)

25 M Hammer, *The Reengineering Revolution* (Harper Collins, 1995)

26 JP Kotter, 'Leading change: Why transformation efforts fail', *Harvard Business Review* (1995), https://hbr.org/1995/05/leading-change-why-transformation-efforts-fail-2, accessed 15 February 2023

27 JP Kotter, *Leading Change* (Harvard Business Review Press, 1996)

28 N Nohria and M Beer, 'Cracking the code of change', *Harvard Business Review* (2000), https://hbr.org/2000/05/cracking-the-code-of-change, accessed 15 February 2023

29 T Senturia, L Flees, M Maceda, 'Leading change management requires sticking to the PLOT', Bain & Company (2008), http://docplayer.net/6559720-Leading-change-management-requires-sticking-to-the-plot-by-todd-senturia-lori-flees-and-manny-maceda.html, accessed 15 February 2023

30 C Dewar and S Keller, 'The irrational side of change management', *McKinsey Quarterly* (2009), www.mckinsey.com/capabilities/people-and-organizational-performance/our-insights/the-irrational-side-of-change-management, accessed 15 February 2023

31 C Dewar and S Keller, ibid

32 M Hughes, 'Do 70 per cent of all organizational change initiatives really fail?', *Journal of Change Management*, 11/4 (16 December 2011), 451–464, https://doi.org/10.1080/14697017.2011.630506

33 J Frahm, '70% of change fails: Bollocks!', Agile Change Leadership Institute, Blog (2019), https://aclinstitute.com/70-change-fail, accessed 15 February 2023

34 K Hall, 'Co-op says IT upgrade project going swell since axing IBM', *The Register* (2018), www.theregister.com/2018/04/06/coop_it_upgrade_post_ibm_progress_report, accessed 15 February 2023

35 Co-operative Group Limited, 'The Co-operative Group to retain General Insurance business', co-operative.coop (2014), www.co-operative.coop/media/news-releases/the-co-operative-group-to-retain-general-insurance-business, accessed 15 February 2023

36 Co-operative Group Limited, 'Announcement of an implementation and managed service agreement with IBM', co-operative.coop (2015), www.co-operative.coop/media/news-releases/managed-service-agreement-with-ibm, accessed 15 February 2023

37 Co-operative Group Limited (2015), ibid

38 J Belden, 'Co-op Insurance sues IBM for breach of contract: Is agile at scale worth the risk?', UpperEdge (2018), https://upperedge.com/ibm/co-op-insurance-sues-ibm-for-breach-of-contract, accessed 15 February 2023

39 G Corfield, 'Co-op Insurance and IBM play blame game over collapse of £175m megaproject', *The Register* (2020), www.theregister.com/2020/01/22/co_op_insurance_v_ibm_high_court_trial_project_cobalt, accessed 15 February 2023

40 L Brown, 'UK: Complex, messy and interesting – lessons from the Co-op v IBM dispute', linklaters.com, Blog (2021), www.linklaters.com/en/insights/blogs/digilinks/2021/march/uk---complex-messy-and-interesting, accessed 15 February 2023

41 J Belden (2018), ibid; L Brown (2021), ibid

42 R Bonnar, 'What can the public sector learn from CISGIL v IBM? Part one – the legal lessons', DLA Piper, Blog (2021), https://blogs.dlapiper.com/uk-government-blog/2021/04/what-can-the-public-sector-learn-from-cisgil-v-ibm-part-one-the-legal-lessons, accessed 15 February 2023

43 E Marshall, 'An IT showdown – CIS General Insurance Ltd v IBM United Kingdom Ltd', Browne Jacobson (2021), www.brownejacobson.com/insights/an-it-showdown, accessed 15 February 2023

44 G Corfield (2020), ibid

45 L Brown (2021), ibid

46 E Marshall (2021), ibid

47 E Marshall (2021), ibid

48 R Bonnar (2021), ibid

49 R Bonnar (2021), ibid

50 R Bonnar(2021), ibid (bullet list)

51 G Corfield (2020), ibid

52 Co-operative Group Limited, 'Co-op sells insurance *underwriting* business and starts new partnership with Markerstudy', co-operative.coop (2020), www.co-operative.coop/media/news-releases/co-op-sells-insurance-

underwriting-business-and-starts-new-partnership-with, accessed 15 February 2023

53 W Kirkman, 'Co-op Insurance sees £15.5m pre-tax operating loss in H1 2017', postonline.com (2017), www.postonline.co.uk/insurer/3313541/co-op-insurance-sees-ps11m-h1-loss, accessed 15 February 2023

54 E Beer, 'Co-op Insurance wins £80.6m from IBM for failed IT project', The Stack (2022), https://thestack.technology/co-op-vs-ibm-80m-appeal-win, accessed 15 February 2023

55 S Wynne-Jones, 'Lidl, Kaufland owner increases sales to €133.6bn in 2021', European Supermarket Magazine (2022), www.esmmagazine.com/retail/lidl-kaufland-owner-increases-sales-to-e133-6bn-in-2021-174288, accessed 15 February 2023

56 Consultancy.uk, 'Lidl cancels SAP introduction having sunk €500 million into it', Consultancy.uk (2018), www.consultancy.uk/news/18243/lidl-cancels-sap-introduction-having-sunk-500-million-into-it, accessed 15 February 2023

57 C Saran, 'Lidl dumps €500m SAP project', Computer Weekly (2018), www.computerweekly.com/news/252446965/Lidl-dumps-500m-SAP-project, accessed 5 February 2023

58 A Watton, 'Lidl cancels €500 SAP IT project – 4 learnings to consider', bestpracticegroup.com (2018), www.bestpracticegroup.com/lidl-cancels-e500m-sap-it-project-4-learnings-to-consider, accessed 15 February 2023

59 Consultancy.uk (2018), ibid

60 A Watton (2018), ibid

61 C Saran (2018), ibid; A Watton (2018), ibid

62 Consultancy.uk (2018), ibid

63 A Watton (2018), ibid

64 C Saran (2018), ibid

65 Consultancy.uk (2018), ibid

66 A Watton (2018), ibid

67 H Dolfing, 'Case study 12: Lidl's €500 million SAP debacle', henricodolfing.com (2020), www.henricodolfing.com/2020/05/case-study-lidl-sap-debacle.html, accessed 5 February 2023

68 Consultancy.uk (2018), ibid

69 H Dolfing (2020), ibid

70 H Dolfing (2020), ibid

71 A Watton (2018), ibid

72 H Dolfing (2020), ibid

73   Y Van Looveren, 'Sven Seidel resigns as Lidl CEO', Retail
     Detail (2017), www.retaildetail.eu/news/food/sven-seidel-
     resigns-lidl-ceo, accessed 15 February 2023
74   Consultancy.uk, ibid
75   Lidl GB, 'Lidl GB becomes first UK supermarket to trial
     on-shelf smart refills', Lidl.co.uk (2022), https://corporate.
     lidl.co.uk/media-centre/pressreleases/2022/on-shelf-refill-
     trial, accessed 15 February 2023
76   Entrepreneur, 'Do you have "shiny object" syndrome? What is
     it and how to beat it', *Entrepreneur* (2017), www.entrepreneur.
     com/living/do-you-have-shiny-object-syndrome-what-it-is-
     and-how-to/288370, accessed 11 April 2023
77   A Hayes, 'What is cost-benefit analysis, how is it used,
     what are its pros and cons?', Investopedia.com (2023),
     www.investopedia.com/terms/c/cost-benefitanalysis.asp,
     accessed 2 April 2023
78   J Fernando, 'Return on investment (ROI): How to calculate
     it and what it means', Investopedia.com (2022), www.
     investopedia.com/terms/r/returnoninvestment.asp,
     accessed 15 February 2023
79   J Fernando, 'Internal rate of return (IRR) rule: Definition
     and example', Investopedia.com (2022), www.investopedia.
     com/terms/i/irr.asp, accessed 15 February 2023
80   J Kagan, 'Payback period explained, with the formula
     and how to calculate it', Investopedia (2022), www.
     investopedia.com/terms/p/paybackperiod.asp accessed
     15 February 2023
81   W Kenton, 'Discounted payback period: What it is,
     and how to calculate it', Investopedia (2020), www.
     investopedia.com/terms/d/discounted-payback-period.
     asp, accessed 15 February 2023
82   A Howard, 'Faster horses', adrianhoward.com (2019),
     https://adrianhoward.com/posts/faster-horses, accessed
     15 February 2023
83   The GC Index®, www.thegcindex.com, accessed 15
     February 2023
84   Smooth road, copyright Stefan Mächler/Unsplash
85   Dangerous path, copyright 2022 Ko Zatu/Shutterstock
86   A Kwan, C Stefanita, R Gupta, 'Monitor Deloitte's 2022
     Chief Transformation Officer study: Designing successful
     transformations', Deloitte (2022), p21, www2.deloitte.com/us/
     en/pages/consulting/articles/survey-chief-transformation-
     officers-success.html, accessed 15 February 2023

Interesting Reading

Here are a few excellent reads relating to transformational change, human behaviour and decision making:

Adam Alter, *Drunk Tank Pink: And other unexpected forces that shape how we think, feel, and behave* (Penguin, 2014)

Daniel Kahneman, Olivier Sibony, Cass R. Sunstein, *Noise* (William Collins, 2021)

Daniel Kahneman, *Thinking, Fast and Slow* (Penguin, 2012)

Dr Tammy Watchorn, *The Change Ninja Handbook: An interactive adventure for leading change* (Practical Inspiration Publishing, 2022)

Mariana Mazzucato and Rosie Collington, *The Big Con: How the consulting industry weakens our businesses, infantilizes our governments and warps our economies* (Allen Lane, 2023)

Robert I Sutton, *Weird Ideas That Work: How to build a creative company* (Free Press, 2007)

Jane Logie, *Getting Transformation Right: A leader's guide to the management of change at scale* (Rethink Press, 2021)

Richard Chataway, *The Behaviour Business: How to apply behavioural science for business success* (Harriman House, 2020)

David Eagleman, *The Brain: The story of you* (Canongate, 2016)

Rolf Dobelli, *The Art of Thinking Clearly: Better thinking, better decisions* (Sceptre, 2014)

Acknowledgements

I would like to thank the brilliant people I've worked with over the years – the breadth and depth of their knowledge and experience has been invaluable and has given me the opportunity to learn and grow and made this book possible. I am also very fortunate to be part of some amazing groups full of incredibly talented professionals:

- Camelot – connecting the world of insurance (www.camelotmarketplace.com)

- The Digital Transformation People (www. thedigitaltransformationpeople.com)

- The Transformation Leaders Hub (www. thetransformationleadershub.com)

My beta readers deserve special mention and huge thanks as their feedback and comments helped me improve my material immeasurably – David Clamp, Shân Millie, Tony Tarquini, Hélène Stanway, Mark Simpson, Karen Stanford, Tim Ellis, Tony Lockwood, Paul Higgins, Karen Hogg, Alex Hall, Nicola White, Lesley Townsend, and my fabulously talented wife, Lisa, who read more draft versions that I ever thought possible to produce.

Huge thanks as well to Philippa Harrod from Bright Lights Business Services (www.teambrightlights.com), who helped me with the research, sourcing images and producing the diagrams for the book, and also to Dr John Mervyn-Smith, Simon Etherington, Nathan Ott and Nicole Rogers from the GC Index® (www.thegcindex.com) for their support and permission to use the images in Chapter Nine, and to Gemma Roszkowski of hiddengemdesign (www.hiddengemdesign.com) for producing them.

Manjit Sohal from Sohal Light Photography (www.sohallight.photography) took my photo. Alex Durham from Vavavoom Videos (www.vavavoomvideos.com) created the videos that accompany the book as well as some of the promotional material together with Martin Whiskin (voiceover artist), Niall Carney (motion designer) and Alissia Clifton (copywriter). The team at Rethink Press supported me throughout the writing and publishing process.

Last, but by no means least, thank you to WPClipart (www.wpclipart.com), who provide copyright-free artwork – it's one of their images that I use for the Rabbits From Hats logo.

The Author

 Gary has worked in the change and transformation space since 1996, initially as a consultant for Computer Sciences Corporation (now DXC Technology), providing enterprise workflow, customer relationship management (CRM) and document management solutions to companies in the insurance industry.

He has subsequently worked across a range of industries in a variety of project and programme roles and head of change positions in the UK and overseas for the likes of AIG, Aon, Colt Technology Services, Direct Line Group, European Financial Data Services (now IFDS), Lloyds Banking Group, Post Office Insurance,

Talbot Underwriting (now part of AIG), Thames Water, Wipro and Xchanging (now DXC Technology).

Gary has turned around failing programmes and successfully delivered multimillion-pound transformation initiatives, implementing new systems, operating models and ways of working. He has guest lectured on transformational change at Surrey University and is a member of Mensa*.

In 2015, Gary founded *Rabbits From Hats*** providing transformational change advisory and consulting services. He works with business leaders and organisations to help them better understand transformational change so it can be approached in the right way and executed and delivered successfully.

For further information, you can get in touch with Gary on LinkedIn or through the Rabbits From Hats website.

in www.linkedin.com/in/
gary-burke-transformational-change

www.rabbitsfromhats.co.uk

---

* https://mensa.org.uk
** A tongue-in-cheek name that reflects the unrealistic expectations organisations can sometimes have regarding transformational change – rabbits really are expected to be pulled from hats!